Three Years from "Thirty"

A Play

by Mike O'Malley

A Samuel French Acting Edition

FOUNDED 1830

New York Hollywood London Toronto
SAMUELFRENCH.COM

Copyright © 1996 by Mike O'Malley

ALL RIGHTS RESERVED

CAUTION: Professionals and amateurs are hereby warned that *THREE YEARS FROM "THIRTY"* is subject to a Licensing Fee. It is fully protected under the copyright laws of the United States of America, the British Commonwealth, including Canada, and all other countries of the Copyright Union. All rights, including professional, amateur, motion picture, recitation, lecturing, public reading, radio broadcasting, television and the rights of translation into foreign languages are strictly reserved. In its present form the play is dedicated to the reading public only.

The amateur live stage performance rights to *THREE YEARS FROM "THIRTY"* are controlled exclusively by Samuel French, Inc., and licensing arrangements and performance licenses must be secured well in advance of presentation. PLEASE NOTE that amateur Licensing Fees are set upon application in accordance with your producing circumstances. When applying for a licensing quotation and a performance license please give us the number of performances intended, dates of production, your seating capacity and admission fee. Licensing Fees are payable one week before the opening performance of the play to Samuel French, Inc., at 45 W. 25th Street, New York, NY 10010.

Licensing Fee of the required amount must be paid whether the play is presented for charity or gain and whether or not admission is charged.

Stock licensing fees quoted upon application to Samuel French, Inc.

For all other rights than those stipulated above, apply to: Mr. Sheldon R. Lubliner, Professional Artists, 513 West 54th Street, New York, NY 10019.

Particular emphasis is laid on the question of amateur or professional readings, permission and terms for which must be secured in writing from Samuel French, Inc.

Copying from this book in whole or in part is strictly forbidden by law, and the right of performance is not transferable.

Whenever the play is produced the following notice must appear on all programs, printing and advertising for the play: "Produced by special arrangement with Samuel French, Inc."

Due authorship credit must be given on all programs, printing and advertising for the play.

ISBN 978-0-573-69597-1   Printed in U.S.A.   #22704

No one shall commit or authorize any act or omission by which the copyright of, or the right to copyright, this play may be impaired.

No one shall make any changes in this play for the purpose of production.

Publication of this play does not imply availability for performance. Both amateurs and professionals considering a production are *strongly* advised in their own interests to apply to Samuel French, Inc., for written permission before starting rehearsals, advertising, or booking a theatre.

No part of this book may be reproduced, stored in a retrieval system, or transmitted in any form, by any means, now known or yet to be invented, including mechanical, electronic, photocopying, recording, videotaping, or otherwise, without the prior written permission of the publisher.

IMPORTANT BILLING AND CREDIT REQUIREMENTS

All producers of THREE YEARS FROM "THIRTY" *must* give credit to Mike O'Malley in all programs distributed in connection with performances of the Play and in all instances in which the title of the Play appears for purposes of advertising, publicizing or otherwise exploiting the Play and/or a production. The name Mike O'Malley *must* also appear on a separate line, on which no other name appears, immediately following the title, and *must* appear in size of type not less than fifty percent the size of the title type.

AUTHOR'S DEDICATION:

THREE YEARS FROM "THIRTY" would not have been possible, without the support of hundreds of people who gave their time, their support, their encouragement, their guidance, their hard work, their acting, their love, and their money. To these friends, and to the wonderful people who filled the seats of the Sanford Meisner theater and bought tickets to the show, this play is dedicated.

THREE YEARS FROM "THIRTY" premiered at the
Sanford Meisner Theater on
November 8, 1994.

Production credits were the following:

THREE YEARS FROM "THIRTY"
a new play
by Mike O'Malley

Directed by John Znidarsic

Cast:
(in alphabetical order)
Jim Barry as Bart
Jack Carey as Bob
Victoria Labalme as Ashley
Richard Munroe as Victor
Mike O'Malley as Tom
Jackie Phelan/Dani Kline as Stephanie
Marla Sucharetza as Jessica

The set was designed by Stuart Rosenstein
The lighting was designed by Deborah Constantine
Stage Managed by Darren Matthew Bycoff
Production Coordinated by Samantha Osby

Presented by:
Psi/Clone Entertainment, Inc.
in association with Limmerance Faction
Executive Producer: James Bethea
Produced by Stuart Rosenstein

ACT I

Scene 1

(The lights come up on a man in his late twenties who is wearing a brown uniform from the United Parcel Service. He is standing on a street corner in Boston, Massachusetts. It is twilight, and he holds a bouquet of daisies in one hand, and in his other hand, a cellular phone. This man is Tom Gannon.)

TOM. Mrs. Titus? Tom here. Tom Gannon... Yes. Hi... I'm fine--excellent actually. Oh, hold on! I'm losing you here... *(He moves his body around to find a clearer frequency.)* Mrs. Titus? There. Oh no--it's a cellular phone. What? No, I'm far from rich. *(Laughs.)* This is my work phone. You know, with UPS, I'm on the road a lot. *(Beat.)* Still with UPS, yes. But those teaching prospects look good. And your daughter keeps me optimistic and happy. Well it's been six years, I hope so... Uh huh. *(Laughs.)* Listen Mrs. Titus, I tried your husband at work, but I couldn't get through to him. Well, frankly, the reason I called is... I was wondering what you and Mr. Titus were doing tomorrow...

(The lights fade on TOM and come up on JESSICA TITUS. JESSICA, who is TOM'S girlfriend, paces around in his apartment. The apartment looks like a page out of Fraternity 101. Beer posters on the walls, a framed photo of Fenway Park, etc. She's wearing Tom's Boston University sweatshirt as she paces, holding the telephone.)

JESSICA. Hi. Jack Titus please. It's his daughter. *(Beat.)* Hi Daddy! I'm okay. Yeah. No. Really. How's Mom? Great. No, really... I'm great. Well, I had an audition for a commercial, and I'm waiting to hear on that. Two weeks ago. Sometimes they look at a lot of people though. And I just auditioned for a play over at B.U. No, they let alumni audition. Uh-huh... Yeah. Uh-huh. Tom called you? Hmmph. What about? No. When? He called you at work? I have no idea. No. He should be home soon. I'm actually here right now. His roommate was here. Dad, I was wondering... *(Beat.)* not a lot. Not a lot. Dad. Daddy I know. Dad, it's... yes. Yes I know. Dad I'm trying. I'm just... *(She's frustrated, and begins to get teary.)* I'm okay, I really am. Yes. Yes. Yes. There's only so -yes. I'm just really at a low point. I know. Thanks Dad. I really appreciate it. I'll pay you back. I'm--yeah. Okay. I love you too. Okay, me too. Bye. *(She hangs up phone and says aloud:)* I'm pathetic.

(After she hangs up the phone, she puts her head in her hands and sighs, and then starts to move towards the kitchen. Then the front door swings open and Tom enters, carrying the bouquet of daisies. He's "on top of the world," and enters with sincere, playful enthusiasm.)

TOM. Birthday girl? B-B-B-B-B-Birthday girl! There she is... Kiss me baby.
JESSICA. You finish your route early?
TOM. Yeah, I kept telling myself, "The faster I deliver, the faster I get to kiss her." I missed you last night. My lips are needing some attention.

(She pecks him on the lips.)

TOM. Okay, goodnight Mom! I miss the passion too Mom.

JESSICA. *(Catching the hint.)* I'm sorry, I'm not having a very stellar day. I'm just--uhgh--I feel so pathetic. I just begged my Dad for money.

TOM. What's a Dad for?

JESSICA. What's that supposed to mean?

TOM. Guys love that shit, providing, helping... Besides, you need that money more than he does.

JESSICA. I shouldn't be calling home for money.

TOM. *(Consoling.)* Hey, so things are slow in you career, and your family helped out, so what?

JESSICA. No, they've helped me out enough. Too much. What the hell am I doing?

TOM. Hey, hey... buddy, don't beat yourself up here.

JESSICA. No, it's just... look at me... It's well past the time to stand on my own. And regarding my career, it's past slow. I think I'm regressing. *(She pauses, frustrated with herself.)* I've had this great upbringing and I've had these great opportunities and this great education, and I've squandered them, and turned into this whining, inactive loser.

TOM. You are not a loser. You got me. Big winner. We're talking big jackpot O'guy.

JESSICA. Did you know that Mimi Plankton has a TV show?

TOM. Who?

JESSICA. Mimi Plankton Tom? Mimi Plankton! Remember? At school, she played the obnoxious waif in "Godspell."

TOM. Big lips?
JESSICA. Exactly. Do you know she has a TV show!?
TOM. Ah-no, I didn't.
JESSICA. Her picture's in <u>Vanity Fair!</u> Look!

(She hands him a copy of <u>Vanity Fair</u> magazine.)

TOM. She looks hot.
JESSICA. What?
TOM. I'm joking with you. Why are you so upset?
JESSICA. Mimi Plankton on TV! Talk about the definitive premonition of the Apocalypse! She was a cheerleader. *(Beat.)* I knew I should have gone to L.A.
TOM. Hold on here. Please. Let's not go down this conversation road today.
JESSICA. No, it's just that—
TOM. *(Seriously.)* You know that the only fellowship I got was here in Boston. I did not force you to stay, Jess.
JESSICA. I know.
TOM. We did this for us.
JESSICA. I know, I know, I'm sorry, I'm just, I'm sorry, I'm, I'm just feeling sorry for myself. I hate this. Uh. I'm sorry.
TOM. It's okay...

(She kisses him.)

JESSICA. Hey, did you call my Dad today?
TOM. Uh-ya. Did he--why do --did he call back?
JESSICA. I just spoke to him--he said you called.
TOM. *(Deflecting.)* Yeah. I couldn't get through to him. Yeah, yeah. You know, since I'm applying for some teaching jobs, I thought I'd finally take him up on his offer to write me

a couple of recommendations, and uh, I thought he'd write a perfect letter to this superintendent down in Providence--I don't know, who knows, you know, people seem to be impressed with letters that are signed with "Professor."

JESSICA. Providence?

TOM. Yeah!! It's like a forty minute drive from here. There's a job available that combines coaching varsity soccer and track and teaching 10th grade world history. How perfect is that? I could commute for a while, and then we could, you know, maybe move there. How great is that?

JESSICA. Providence, Rhode Island?

TOM. Jess, I've totally checked it out. I did a little reconnaissance mission. Outside the city area, it's really nice, it's close to the beach, and check it out, they've got a repertory theater there that's totally legit, and it's supposed to be pretty good. They did... what was it... I saw something on this flyer— Oh yeah! Last year they did "Waiting for Goat!"

JESSICA. Godot. "Waiting for Godot." Tom, I'm not moving to Providence, Rhode Island. Number one, it's not exactly a hotbed of entertainment opportunities.

TOM. But I kinda thought...

JESSICA. What?

TOM. I thought you were sort of—

JESSICA. What!?

TOM. I just, you know, the whole idea of going to New York or L.A. and being in the movies, I thought you were giving up—

JESSICA. You think I'm giving up?!

TOM. I, uh—

JESSICA. I'm not giving up!

TOM. Okay.

JESSICA. "Okay!?" I am not giving up! You try it Tom. You try to get a goddamned acting job, let alone an audition in this town. And this is Boston. What do you think it'll be like in Providence? *(Beat.)* I don't see you with a teaching job!

TOM. So what are you saying?

JESSICA. Nothing.

TOM. What? Say it.

JESSICA. You're being oversensitive.

TOM. Jess, believe it or not it is not easy to find a good teaching job.

JESSICA. A specific teaching job.

TOM. What? Okay, yes. A place where I want to work. And help. And coach. And teach. And not settle. Hell Jess, gimme some slack time. I don't officially get my degree until Christmas! And you know I've only sent out 8 or 9 resumes. I'm looking! You think I enjoy getting out of bed everyday so I can get in a brown truck and deliver brown boxes in this fashionably hip and attractive suit of "brown-ness."

JESSICA. You took the job.

TOM. I needed the benefits. I'm not on Daddy's insurance. *(Beat.)* I'm sorry. I didn't mean that. Jess, we've been over this a gazillion times. It's just... I can't take any job. Look at me *(Playful.)* Aside from being incredibly handsome and charming and having a beautiful body you can't keep your hands off of--I've done nothing with my life--I've given nothing. Look at my life: I've got a college education, I'm finishing up my masters that I got a scholarship for, I've got a great group of friends that are important to me, my health, and most importantly, I got you. Now it's time to get into the trenches and start attacking the problems--Urban public schools are a warzone. Don't you see? Remember that book I was just reading about those soldiers at D-Day? They were volunteers, those D-Day guys, they believed in something. They lived and died for something. I'm not even close to having an equivalent. What have I done? I've struggled for nothing! I want to get in there and do something important!! I want to be able to tell my kids I did something a little more noble than "Well son, when I was a young man--I sent a couple E-mails, hit the Stairmaster and did my ab routine!" Public schools pay alright for what I need now. And, even if I could follow through on some contacts, going off to coach soccer at some country club prep school is not my idea of a challenge. Call me crazy.

JESSICA. Tom, I don't think you're crazy. *(Softly.)* I admire you for going after what you want.

TOM. And, don't forget, you admire me for my addictive charisma. Of which you are the most frequent and fortunate benefactor... *(Kisses her.)* I'm telling you, I got a good feeling about the immediate future. For both of us. And there's plenty of time to talk about it and cut and paste and figure it all out, right? *(He kisses her.)* Look, the guys should be back soon. Let's all go out for dinner or something.

JESSICA. I can't. I mean, I would, but, Stephanie Pelliteer's in town.

TOM. *(Surprised.)* Really? Wow, what is she doing?

JESSICA. I don't know. She left me a message. We've been playing phone tag for the last eleven months, but this time, she said she's going to her folks place on the Cape... so she's coming through Boston. I'm really psyched to see her. She said she had news. Maybe she got engaged to Mark.

TOM. *(Sarcastic.)* Lucky Mark.

JESSICA. Okay, don't start. *(Beat.)* So, I'm gonna go and... I'll see you tomorrow.

TOM. Big birthday girl tomorrow! Twenty-seven!
JESSICA. Don't remind me.
TOM. What? *(Playfully.)* You look nineteen. Well, stop by if you wanna sleep over.
JESSICA. Okay, but... we'll probably be up late talking.

(She moves to leave.)

TOM. Uh-oh, I can see it now, red wine, cigarettes, Caesar salads--don't overdo it you crazy ladies. *(Beat.)* Well, I'll miss you. And, don't forget your amazingly beautiful and sweet smelling flowers.
JESSICA. Oh, yeah. Thanks. So, what are you going to do?
TOM. Whatever. The guys should be home soon. Boys night out I guess.
JESSICA. I can see it now. Pitchers, stogies, cheeseburgers—
TOM. Somebody has to perpetuate the stereotype on this end.
JESSICA. Okay... Well, bye!

(She starts to leave.)

TOM. Hey! Come here. *(He kisses her.)* That's better. Bye.
JESSICA. Bye.

(She exits, and TOM walks over to the stereo and cranks up a tune, then cracks a beer as he begins to sort through the mail. As he does this, BOB RUTHERFORD, his roommate, enters from his bedroom dressed in nothing but boxer shorts

and black socks, carrying a bong, and looking like he just woke up.)

BOB. Dude, what's up?

TOM. Bob! Were you sleeping in there? Sorry about that man.

BOB. What time is it?

TOM. 5:40.

BOB. Whoa. I was comatose in there.

TOM. Hung?

BOB. Like dung. I got so lit last night. *(As he continues to speak, he begins packing the bong.)* It was epic. After I played "The Oyster Shanty" we started off with beers at "The Embassy," then we did shooters over at "The Black Rose," then ended up at "The Beacon Hill Pub" doing funnels.

TOM. Aren't you getting a little too old to be sucking back funnels?

BOB. First off, I ain't old. More importantly, they were free.

(Suddenly the door swings open, and in through the door arrives BART VOWERS, TOM'S other roommate. He is a stock broker in his late twenties who has adopted a men's fashion magazine attitude to go with his affected swagger. Dressed in a slick suit, and dangling his briefcase, he enters the room with an extra air of confidence. All of this aura, however, does not mask his genuine charm, which can still shine through the presentation.)

BART. Boys, do I look any different to you today? Are you feeling any different in my presence?

(BOB takes his mouth away from the bong and blows out some smoke.)

BOB. No different that usual Dude.
TOM. What's up with you, Smirky?
BART. This roommate of yours, this man in front of you, this mofo, nailed his first serious account today and I'm flying to New York City on Monday to finalize the details!
TOM. There it is!
BOB. Way to bag the cash Bucko.
BART. Boys, follow me on this one. If I get this deal I will have a direct path to one of the leading human beings shepherding the information superhighway towards bold new galactic destinations.
TOM. Way to go man!

(They all slap high fives, etc.)

BOB. Well well, so Wally Wall Street scores big.
TOM. The money-maker!

(BOB and TOM laugh.)

BART. Laugh it up boys. While you sit back in your retro-active, hi-fi, eight track cartridge world, I will be approaching financial greatness at light speed. Enough talk. Time to celebrate.

(BART walks over to the kitchen, grabs 3 shot glasses, sets them up on the coffee table and majestically pulls out a bottle of Jaegermeister.)

TOM. Whoa! Way too early for Jaegermeister pal.
BART. When did that ever stop us?
BOB. Bart, it's not even six o'clock.
BART. C'mon guys!! We're going out tonight! I'm not going to drink this alone. Guys... c'mon. Never say nay to Jae!!
TOM. Line 'em up.
BOB. It's not like I have to be anywhere tomorrow.
BART. Bob, has there ever been a tomorrow where you actually had to be somewhere specific?
BOB. Uh...
TOM. Drink with me. *(They all hoist the shots and throw them back.)* Well, I tell you boys where I gotta be tomorrow! I'm driving up to Springfield to get the thumbs up from Jessica's Dad.
BOB. You're going through with it?
TOM. Of course I'm going through with it!! I just gotta do the rap with her dad before I pop the question officially.
BOB. Why don't you just ask her yourself?
BART. Yeah Tom, who does that ask-the-father-first formality anymore?
TOM. Guys, did it ever occur to you that Jessica's family has some traditional beliefs?
BOB/BART. No.
TOM. Do you think I'd still be living with you two jackasses if Jessica's parents could deal with premarital cohabitation?
BART/BOB. Yes.
TOM. Sorry guys, I love ya, but it's time to move on. It's not like it's a big surprise after six years. It's a given... And call me crazy, but I'm just really fired up to have a wife, and start a family and you know, just leap into adulthood with her.

BART. Hey, Crazy. Before you make this majestic leap, you gotta ask her Dad? Come on Tom.

TOM. Look. I'm not asking his permission, I'm respectfully asking for his blessings. Sometimes, you gotta respect tradition. Besides, it's a done deal. The guy loves me. *(Laughs.)* I mean, c'mon, you think he'll say no?

BOB/BART. Well...

TOM. Funny.

BART. Well, if he does say yes, are you gonna sign a pre-nup?

TOM. A what?

BOB. A pre-nuptial agreement.

TOM. Yeah, that's the first thing on my list after I give her the ring.

BART. You may jest in sarcasm Tommy, but you gotta cover your ass these days.

TOM. Come on!!

BOB. Tom, you gotta admit, chicks are totally unpredictable. They're in love one day, next day Kaboom! Bye bye love, hello horniness.

TOM. Jess and I have a great sex life!

BART. That's what his stepbrother thought too.

TOM. What?

BOB. I told you this.

TOM. Told me what?

BART. About his step brother's marriage nightmare.

TOM. What?

BOB. My step-bro thought his wife was well oiled and provided for until she totally bailed on him after eight years of marriage. Just like your basic low rent hotel room, porno flick, she turned thirty-five, menopause was beckoning, she knew she was drying up downstairs—

TOM. *(To BART.)* His graphics always enhance his story.
BART. Sh... listen.
BOB. So she's actually far from well oiled... she's seeing the crow's feet in the mirror upstairs and she's feeling the dry heat—
TOM/BART. Downstairs.
BOB. Exactly. So what does she do?
TOM. I don't know, what?
BOB. She shacks up with the landscaping guy.
TOM. What does this have to do with me?
BART. The landscaper Tom!! After eight years of marriage she has an affair with the guy her husband is paying seventeen bucks an hour to trim the hedges!
TOM. And spread his fertilizer.
BOB. You wouldn't be laughing if it happened to you.
BART. But the real story Tom—
BOB. The real story is my step bro catches venereal warts from his wife!
BART. Crotch warts, Tom!
TOM. Well... it's not AIDS—
BOB. It's not crabs or cancer either, but it is kinda sick to catch warts from your wife.
TOM. True, but not as bad as catching them from some immigrant Indonesian hooker after a Red Sox game.

(TOM and BOB look at BART.)

BART. That was a very long time ago on a very drunk night.
BOB/TOM. Sure it was.
BART. Hey, I'm human.
TOM. We're still breaking down the DNA.

BOB. Bottom line though Tom, it was too much of a shocker for my brother to deal with, so he divorced her and in the process, lost his house and his boat and now, he's the one making alimony payments.

BART. No pre-nup! Better or worse bullshit.

BOB. Exactly. Times have changed. I don't think when the vows were invented they envisioned somebody inheriting a patchwork of VD warts from the guy who operated a leaf blower.

TOM. You guys are just trying to bust my balls. I have enough faith and trust in Jess that she won't pass on some genital fungus she got from some landscaper.

BART. Tom, you may laugh, but hey Tom, you're the UPS guy. You're hip—

BOB. Cool—

BART. You get propositioned by lonely ladies...

BOB. 24-7.

BART. Working men like yourself are desirable in the new millennium, could be a landscaper—

BOB. Plumber—

BART. UPS guy—

BOB. Your buddy from work--what's his name?

BART. Perfect example. Vinny.

BOB. Vinny.

TOM. Vinny wouldn't sleep with his buddy's wife.

BOB. That shit happens all the time.

BART. All the time Tom.

TOM. Why would I want to curse my marriage with some legal document that--what? Allows me to keep myself--what? Financially secure if for some unforeseen reason we divorce, which we won't. So I get to keep half of my IRA that's worth

12 grand or I get my car with 70,000 miles on it--who gives a shit? I'm not looking for a way to cover my ass. I'm not looking for an out. I want in. This is the real, real thing. Besides, what do I have to protect? It was just two months ago that I paid off the Visa balance I "cha chinged" up to two grand Spring Break Senior Year. *(Sarcastic.)* That's quite a financial portfolio to protect eh? The only thing I own are clothes and memories.

BART. Point taken.
BOB. Point taken. Let's get lit.
TOM. Done.
BART. Does Jessica know you're finally going to propose?
TOM. No! There's gotta be some mystery to it.
BART. Bold!
BOB. Scary.
TOM. Secure dudes. Secure.
BART. When are you going to do it?
TOM. Her surprise birthday party tomorrow night.
BOB. Nice.
BART. Well, that's if her Dad says yes.
TOM. He better. Check this out.

(He pulls out a beautiful diamond engagement ring.)

BOB. Solid.
BART. How the hell did you afford that?
TOM. What do you mean, how? Look at my uniform. You think UPS is my dream life?
BART. You look good in brown.
BOB. This is intense Tom. That thing's huge.
TOM. I can't wait till tomorrow! Ahhhhh!
BOB. We're gonna gig so hard tonight!

BART. So, you gonna sign a pre-nup?
BOB. Yeah, have you heard the story—
TOM. You guys are killing me with comedy here...

(They all laugh.)

BOB. We're just giving you shit.
TOM. Well, now that my buddies have shown such belief in the survival of my sacrament of Holy Matrimony... I want to know if you would share the honor of being my co-best men in my wedding.
BOB. Dude, of course!
BART. Tom, I'd be honored man.
TOM. You guys are great friends.
BART. For life man.
BOB. Hell ya! Let's get outta here and get lit! We got celebrating to do!
TOM. Alright, let me change.
BOB. For who? You're getting married.
BART. Yeah, and it's the fall season. I hear brown's coming back.
TOM. Let's get lit.
BART. Get lit!
BOB. Dude get lit!
TOM. Get lit.

(They exit, as the lights go down.)

Scene 2

(Lights up on JESSICA'S apartment. The decor is classy yet inexpensive. STEPHANIE PELLITEER, 27, and ASHLEY GRENTON, also 27, join JESSICA in preparing dinner.)

ASHLEY. You look great!
STEPH. Thanks!
JESSICA. Really, you look fantastic! And skinny... my God. What have you been doing the last three years, fasting? *(Laughs.)*
STEPH. No, no. Oh, no, I'm "Active Woman!" It's my new identity. Activity. Being active. Active, well, maybe not. Hell, when you backpack Asia and catch malaria, you're bound to lose a few.
ASHLEY. I forgot about that. Are you in remission?
STEPH. Yeah, I've got a few more chemo treatments.
ASHLEY. Oh my God, Steph. Well, you hair looks good.
STEPH. Ashley. It was a joke. I'm fine. It's malaria, not cancer.
ASHLEY. Oh. *(Beat.)* Well, anyway, I want you to know that you're my idol. All I've ever wanted to do is like, travel.
STEPH. Travel will beat on your body, that's for sure. I'm a hard-core weather beaten woman. I'm ready for all diseases. Well, I take that back, not all diseases.
JESSICA. So, hold on. You're suddenly in Boston. You leave me a message. What's the news, come on...
STEPH. I'm getting some stuff at my parents' house before I move.
ASHLEY. You're moving back! Yeah!

JESSICA. Wait a minute... backtrack. You and Mark were touring China, la di da, then, you were moving to Aspen to be ski bums, and then a year later you show up here.

ASHLEY. Steph, what's up, come on? Fill us in.

STEPH. What are those looks for? Things are going according to plan. I am in control. Seriously. See--look at this book I'm reading. "Care of the Soul." Ladies, stop whatever you're reading and consume this book.

ASHLEY. That good, huh?

STEPH. It blows "The Road Less Traveled" away. I have found a path for my soul's fulfillment. Plain and simple, I was sick of feeling direction-less. I finally stopped waxing philosophical about what I was going to do and did it. I mean, what was I thinking? I'm living in Aspen, flipping burgers, and composing a screenplay for "Atlas Shrugged." Come on!!! Talk about living in a void!

ASHLEY. A void? Sounds like paradise. I need to be, someplace like, you know, there. Somewhere... there. See, if I had something like that, my life would be set.

STEPH. Believe me you wouldn't be.

JESSICA. Is Mark still in Aspen?

STEPH. Oh, yeah. I didn't tell you?

JESSICA. Tell me what?

ASHLEY. Tell us what?

STEPH. Oh, we're over.

ASHLEY. I thought you were engaged!

JESSICA. *(Concerned.)* What happened?

STEPH. No, Pleeeeaaaase. I'm fine. I broke it off. Shocking I know. First bold decision in my life. But ladies, it was pointless. There I was on the road to J. Crew/Mountain Bike hell and my number was called.

JESSICA. *(Shocked.)* So, it's over! Like, over-over?
STEPH. Over.
ASHLEY. What happened? You guys seemed so great together.
JESSICA. Steph—
STEPH. I just suddenly knew it was time to end it. And you know what? People change. People evolve. No biggie.
JESSICA. You didn't really think about it?
STEPH. Of course I thought about it, I'm no some colossal bitch or anything. It was just, corny as it sounds, like, a vision. Like a huge reality meteor exploding in the midst of my denial.
ASHLEY. Denial of what?
STEPH. My goals, my life. I mean, I'm in the backseat because why? Because he wants to pursue his Swiss Family Robinson ski chalet tree house dream? No. I'm no Swiss Miss. And, I don't hate him for it. I'm just accepting the way my particular road forked, you know?
JESSICA. How did you know it was the right decision though? Not that I'm doubting you or--it's just you guys were together a long time and—
STEPH. Well, I don't know... I don't really, well, okay... Here's the nutshell--one night in Aspen, this is still so clear, over this fettucine alfredo dinner with garlic bread, Van Morrison in the background, raspberry/apple-cinnamon potpourri burning on the stove, this huge fat purple candle dripping wax everywhere, but worth it, you know, for the serious romantic illumination factor... and two bottles of red wine thank you... I'm looking at Mark and listening to him rave, so excited, as he talked about this new snowboard he was saving up for, and how he was going to "thrash" the slopes all winter

and won't it be great to own a surf shop someday... and I'm looking at his face as he's rubbing his brand new goatee he was so proud of—

JESSICA. A goatee!!!???

ASHLEY. I love goatees.

JESSICA. Oh yuck. You're kidding me right?

ASHLEY. I love facial hair!

JESSICA. Ugh! It's like kissing a brillo pad.

ASHLEY. I think it's sexy.

JESSICA. Pseudo hip. No way—

STEPH. Ladies, please. I'm over here. This way. Thank you. Anyway, so I'm looking at Mr. Joe Billy Goat Gruff who I've dated for SIX YEARS and suddenly his mouth is still moving, but I can't hear him. All I can hear is this record skipping in my mind--my own voice echoing itself "Is this the one? Is this the one? Is this the one?" It was eerie. And I knew right then that we were over.

ASHLEY. What do you mean? Is this the one what?

JESSICA. (*Making a connection.*) The one she wants to spend the rest of her life with.

STEPH. Wake up next to, grow old with! The one I want raising my children to be, what? Snowboard waxers!!!!?? Pleeeeeeaase. Yeah, mother and wife to a family of goateed, snowboard waxing, burger flippers!! Sure. Can you imagine? I mean whew--I just couldn't believe I let it go for that long... what was I thinking?

JESSICA. (*To herself.*) Wow.

STEPH. Free-dom!! I'm telling you--when you know you've made the right choice to do the right thing there's like this euphoria.

JESSICA. How's Mark? Is he like devastated?

STEPH. Mark? Come on! Ski season was just beginning. I was a distraction.

ASHLEY. He was cute!

STEPH. When you see someone everyday pretty soon they just start looking like themselves. Besides, I was not going to let myself be ornamental decoration on a guy's life! Right? Am I right? The love ran its course. No biggie.

JESSICA. How do you feel?

STEPH. Look at me. I'm alive again! I'm following my bliss!! And bliss is New York City.

JESSICA. You're moving to New York?

STEPH. Yes ma'am. I'm dropping a big old tab of some NYC. I got a job doing pharmaceutical sales. And I'm getting relocation costs and everything. And the everything includes free rent for three months in a one bedroom on the Upper West Side with... get this... HARDWOOD FLOORS!!

JESSICA. Hardwood floors.

STEPH. And exposed brick. That would be the biggie, thank you. What more does a woman need to be complete?

ASHLEY. True love.

JESSICA. Oh, please Ashley.

STEPH. I've figured out that you've got to be your own woman, and know what you want before you find, or experience quote, unquote true love.

JESSICA. Yes.

ASHLEY. But you were maintaining a relationship.

STEPH. I want something that grows, not maintains.

ASHLEY. I don't know Steph. All this talk about what you want, what to find, "Care of the Soul," "Making it." Hell, how do you ever really know right? To me it's all a big pain in the ass. I see Bart, moving, "shaking," as he calls it. I am sick of

"to-do" lists, planners, schedules, advertising, office politics. I think about how I spent eighty grand in tuition so I could arm myself with the expertise of bullshitting my way through media planning meetings. I just want to hang, you know? Remember when we'd just hang out--why does it have to be so complicated? Oh, WHATEVER. Whine, whine, whine. I'm not in a concentration camp, right? I'm just thinking out loud anyways... Listen you guys, I told Bart I'd meet him out. He closed some big account and wants to celebrate. So—
    STEPH. Bart's selling?!!!! What!!???
    ASHLEY. Mutual funds.
    STEPH. Bart Vowers!?
    ASHLEY. I know. Don't tell me, I know.
    JESSICA. Ash, I thought we were going to just hang out--just the girls.
    ASHLEY. I know, it's just that Bart's leaving for a week and I just you know, want to see him a little extra before Sunday. He said he's going to be traveling a lot now.
    JESSICA. Alright.
    STEPH. So good to see you!
    ASHLEY. You too. Well, I'll see you later tonight back here. Okay? Okay, bye!

(They all ad lib good-byes and hug as ASHLEY exits.)

    STEPH. *(Leaning into JESSICA in a hushed tone.)* Hold on! Bart Vowers selling stocks?
    JESSICA. Yeah, he did a total 180 when his dad died.
    STEPH. Oh my God, that's right, Ashley left me a message about the funeral. Yikes. How is he?

JESSICA. He's born-again.
STEPH. Christian?
JESSICA. Conservative.
STEPH. Bart? I can't see it. What the hell is next? Has Bob got a job?
JESSICA. Bob's the same. He sells T-shirts at colleges and plays Neil Young covers at open mike nights.

(She audibly sighs.)

STEPH. What's the sigh for?
JESSICA. New York.
STEPH. New York?
JESSICA. Oh, Steph, I don't know. You made a move! You're doing something! I'm going nowhere. It's like--I can't balance anymore. Acting. Tom. I'm still doing volunteer work, so I don't feel too shitty about myself. But that's pathetic in and of itself. These little girls have so much to be upset about and here I am—
STEPH. Oh--you're still at that group home?
JESSICA. One night a week, it's not much. Oh, I don't know. My nice little "have everything life"--It's all snowballed into this mass of confusion. More and more, Tom's plans don't seem to jive with mine and like... these voices creep in: "Where am I going? What exactly am I doing?" These life questions. "Do I want to be married? How many kids?" They were always these like theoretical things I sort of knew I had to answer, but that would be, you know, when I was like this adult woman, like my older sister's age. Well, I turn 27 tomorrow! That was my

sister's age when I used to say to myself "I'll be set by then. That's old." I have to get a move on! I never thought it would get to this. I was just going along, I had this fling, and then all of a sudden I loved him and needed him and I began to alter all of my dreams contingent on us--an acting career in Boston!? What was I thinking?

STEPH. What do you mean? You're acting at that King Arthur-Arabian Knights thing—

JESSICA. The "Medieval Manor??!!" Come on! I'm a singing peasant waitress! I've managed to find an acting job that's one rung lower than dinner theater! I've really made my family proud!! *(Beat.)* It's not just the acting thing. It's us.

STEPH. Do you love him?

JESSICA. I mean--yeah I *love* him.

(Beat.)

STEPH. Listen! This is okay! No biggie! You can work this. It's a warning signal to shake things up! Give your life a jolt! Look, Jess, don't make the mistake I made. Live YOUR life. If you don't like where you are you can change it. That's the beauty of self control.

JESSICA. Yeah, but—

STEPH. No, no, no, you see... Get rid of the buts!!! The word "but" is a channel for negative reinforcement. Energize. Vitalize. Think positive! Be positive. I used to think of life as this bottomless bag of time that I had the rest of eternity to fritter away, hang out, kick back and take it as it comes. It ain't that way.

JESSICA. I need another drink.

STEPH. A celebration drink. First, to following your bliss.

(She lifts a beer as they clink glasses.) Cheers!

(Lights down.)

Scene 3

(Lights up on TOM, as he walks out of the bedroom looking very hungover. BOB comes out as before, with bong in hand. BART then comes through the front door with coffee and a newspaper.)

BOB. Dude, get lit.

TOM. Oh yeah, we demonstrated severe depth last night huh? Pounding beers and smashing cups on our heads. I can't drink like that anymore.

BART. It was like college.

BOB. I was fine until I did that body shot with this chick and she slapped me because I licked her neck. Then I booted in the bathroom.

BART. That's great Bob.

TOM. You booted!?

BOB. Yeah, I horrified that chick! She ran. You know what it made me think of? Remember that party at Kappa SIG, when you and I were chugging that Cuervo and that girl was on her face in the corner by the speaker cranked right in her ear?

TOM. Thank God those days are over.

BOB. Those days are what made us! Never say die boys!

TOM. Die. Movin' on. Marriage says die to drinking. Wives

say die.

BOB. The hell with wives. Not for me boys!! The new sexual revolution is just around the corner!! The cure for AIDS, or at least a vaccine is like, it'll be here in no time. You think I'm gonna miss out on that because I'm married? Hell no. You kiddin me? People are gonna be boffin' like banshees. It'll make the 60's look like the Puritan Age!! Little hotties running around throwing themselves at guys. It's gonna be so sick. It'll be like we stared Armageddon in the face and said "Later days Jerky, I've got some boning to do!!" Think about it. Naked Betties everywhere? I haven't had sex without a condom in like seven years. You kidding me? Riding bareback again? It'll be like a new drug!! Oh man. Sick. Oh ho. I can't even think about it.

TOM. Better get an ice pack and cool down there horndog. I'm over it. Time to settle down and get myself a teaching gig and get myself some roots!

BART. Well, at least you're getting a job Tom.

BOB. Hey Bart, enough with your digs at my lifestyle choice. I'm not going to kowtow to some half-baked economic political ideology that says I gotta work some bullshit job. I've got my plan and it suits me; I'm going to make some cash, get some things together , and I'm just gonna move to Montana, you know, like "Dances with Wolves" country. And I'm just gonna kick back, fall in love with a million cowgirls and gig with my guitar.

BART. And live off the millions you're making on that couch.

TOM. He's selling T-shirts!!

BOB. I'm selling T-shirts!!

BART. Bob, there's gonna be a day when you're gonna have to stop selling Co-ed Naked Lacrosse T-shirts at every school in the Northeast. I'm just being a friend. I just want to wake you up from you lack of clues.

BOB. Listen "Slick," you think you got all the answers just because you're close to making some big sale. Some other bullshit sale. Whoopee. Wahoo. Let me tell you something. Coin brings chaos. My family used to have suitcases of cash. Trust funds, prep schools, all that blue blooded bullshit. And as a result, I got three stepfathers, two stepmothers, and a family full of drunks. Not partiers, drunks. So watch what you want; I think you're the one who needs a clue.

BART. Hey, ease up Bob, I'm just jokin with you!

TOM. Listen sensitive lovebirds, I'd love to sit here and chit chat with you, but the fact is I've got a date with Jessica's parents.

BART. Okay Romeo, good luck. You're leavin' us. The great unknown lies ahead.

TOM. Think I look too casual?

BOB. You look fine.

TOM. Alright. Peace.

BOB. Peace dude. If you change your mind, we'll be here!

TOM. Doubt it. Later.

(Tom exits.)

Bob. Later!
BART. Later!

BOB. Put a fork in him.
BART. He's done.

(Lights down)

Scene 4

(Lights up on BART and STEPHANIE in the men's apartment. JESSICA and ASHLEY are offstage in one of the bedrooms.)

STEPH. So, Bart, I hear you've gone from a major in social work to a stock broking jerk.

BART. Who said that?

STEPH. Bart, I'm kidding with you. It's just, your career path, quite a change from before, huh? Social protests in college and all?

BART. Wait, let's backtrack here. Social protest? Look. The only thing left barking about when we were in school was apartheid. So I did it. Got it out of my system. It didn't affect anybody. I mean, what was I thinking? I'm sleeping in a makeshift shanty because I wanted Exxon to divest from South Africa--Come on!!

STEPH. Hey, Mandela got out of jail and became president. Your involvement helped!

BART. Please Stephanie. Let's not overrate a drunken white young American coed's voluntary three day juice fast in a plywood hut with cable.

STEPH. You had cable in there?

BART. And a microwave...

(Beat.)

STEPH. *(Smiling.)* Alright, you got me. I do wanna say I'm sorry about your Dad.
BART. Hey, you know.
JESSICA. *(Entering from bedroom with ASHLEY, and modeling a new outfit.)* Well, what do you think?
STEPH. Perfect.

(TOM and BOB enter with more beer.)

BOB. More Rolling Rock for the masses!!
TOM. *(Seeing JESSICA.)* Yowsa, who's the smokin babe in the jeans looking pipin' hot?
JESSICA. Ashley picked it out.
BART. *(Aside to TOM.)* You never told me--how'd it go?
TOM. What? Oh her Dad--awesome.
BART. Nervous?
TOM. Yeah, but her Dad was really cool. I'm in.
BART. When you going to ask her?
TOM. Tonight.
BART. Tonight? This man wastes no time!! Psyched for you man.
TOM. Yeah, embracing adulthood, finally.
JESSICA. Thanks for all these gifts you guys. You didn't need to do this. And Steph, I love this stuff from "The Body Shop."
STEPH. Isn't that the greatest place? I just walk in there, walk around and sniff. I'm a sniffing psychotic maniac in that place. Soaps, shampoos, avocado foot scrub. I'm pulling caps off bottles, spraying random patches of skin--people think I've

lost my mind. It's the best place. They recycle, they're completely environmentally conscious, and they don't test on animals.

JESSICA. That's great, cause I will not use any products tested on animals.

BART. Why?

JESSICA. Why? They're defenseless, for one.

BART. Oh--here we go.

JESSICA. What?

BART. Save the white spotted humpback non-smoking lesbian whales!

STEPH. *(Holding up a book.)* Okay, check this book out that I got at the mall. Have you seen this "Book of Provocative Questions?"

JESSICA. What kind of questions Steph?

STEPH. Well, it says questions that are supposed to help people communicate with one another.

TOM. Hey, Bob and Bart!

ASHLEY. This could be fun. Pick a question. Let's communicate.

BOB. Let's fornicate.

BART. Bob, really, grow up.

STEPH. Okay, Question # 10 "Which sex do you think has it easier in our culture?"

BOB. That's simple, chicks.

JESSICA. Women.

ASHLEY. You agree with him?

JESSICA. I was correcting him.

BART. I agree with Bob.

TOM. Holy shit!! The book works!

BART. Women have it easier. No doubt in my mind. They have more options. Look at working moms! They can kick back at home or work and both are acceptable.

JESSICA. To who?

BOB. Society.

STEPH. What society are you living in?

JESSICA. A male dominated one.

BART. What?

TOM. I don't know if domination is the right word.

BOB. Chicks have it so easy they don't even realize it.

JESSICA. What is easy about being abused, discriminated against, and sexually harassed? What's easy about the struggle of single mothers? Having to delegate their love for their kids to a day care worker? Easier? Where does easy come in?

BOB. First off, all chicks aren't mothers.

STEPH. They're women.

BOB. I know they're women Dude. I happen to love women.

STEPH. Well then if that's the case, understand that women are just women Bob, not chicks, babes, tang, or anything else. Following that logic, I am not a "dude."

TOM. Great question to start with.

JESSICA. I think you men are afraid to answer truthfully, because you're afraid to admit the truth that men have it so much easier.

TOM. Easier?

JESSICA. Yes easier!

TOM. Oh yeah... What's easy about prostate cancer?

JESSICA. What does that have to do with our culture?

TOM. Culture?? Lemme tell you about culture. A lot of

famous artists have recently come out and admitted their horrific stories of the prostate. Sharing it has become a sort of therapy. "My prostate, it hurts, brother, hold me."

(TOM, begins to fake like he's crying as he reaches for BOB and BART. They join in for a moment, and then, they all burst out laughing hysterically at themselves.)

JESSICA. Pathetic.
STEPH. Look, Tom why don't you pick the next question?

(STEPH hands TOM the book.)

TOM. Yeah, we'll get a little masculine bent on this. I'm kidding. Let's see. "Do you believe in any sort of a god?"
BART. No way! You can't spend your life looking for comfort in a ritual made up by some drunk monk a thousand years ago!! You gotta live for today!! What are the facts of our world? The religion in this life is money, commerce, cash. And he who masters it, he/she that masters it, wins by achieving financial independence.
TOM. So, Bart, I guess your answer would be: Yes, you believe in the religion of money. As long as you're winning.
BART. Well, not exactly.
BOB. Dude, you don't even know what you think.
BART. Okay Bob Dylan, like you do.
BOB. This Bob is proud to be compared to that Bob.
ASHLEY. Oh you're so much cuter that Bob Dylan.
BART. Ashley!

ASHLEY. Well, he is.

BOB. Yeah Dude, I'm a post-modern, cute Bob Dylan!! And you know your comparison is sort of appropriate for this question, because Dylan was a god of sorts. He was this poet who like rose out of the ashes, this phoenix who rose out of the ashes of Buddy Holly's rock and roll roots and transformed music to the folk message of the turbulent 60's. "Mr. Tambourine Man." "Blowin in the Wind." That shit's heavy dude. Have you ever listened to that?

(BOB picks up his guitar.)

BART. We live with you.

TOM. Bart, what is your deal with the sixties?

BART. I just think it's so bogus. Nostalgic reflection to a bullshit generation. There's a generation for you. And Bob, and people like Bob waste their lives by trying to vogue out some Aquarian crap that looked cool on some documentary about the "Mama's and the Papa's."

(BOB begins to sing a popular sixties song as BART mockingly, joins in.)

TOM. Hey guys, give it a rest.

ASHLEY. C'mon, we never get to hear Bob sing.

STEPH. It's kinda like out own "MTV Unplugged."

BOB *(Proudly.)* BOB Unplugged!!

ASHLEY. Keep playing, I like it.

BOB. I'm playing next Tuesday at "The Oyster Shanty!"

ASHLEY. I'll definitely come!
BOB. Thanks Ashley. Nobody ever comes to my shows.
BART. Why pay to see what we hear in our living room?
ASHLEY. It's called supporting your friends.
TOM. Bob, I go when I'm not working second shift, you know that.
ASHLEY. I'll get everybody together. We can all go together. *(Grabbing the book.)* Okay, my turn. Here's one. Wow. This one's tough.
BART. Just read it. Make your personal comment later.
BOB. Bart, lighten up.
ASHLEY. *(To BART.)* Soooorrry. Jeez... Mr. Testy. Okay. If you and your spouse knew before the first trimester that your child would be severely retarded, would you still have it?
TOM. *(Deadpan.)* Well, this book is a barrel of laughs.
ASHLEY. Steph, you go first.
STEPH. No way. There's too much they'll never understand.
TOM. What?
STEPH. They'll never experience a quality of life like normal people.
TOM. What is a "normal" quality of life? What? I don't get it. Are you saying because their brains might be a little slow, their lives aren't worth anything?
BART. Well, when you look at Bob...
BOB. Ha ha.
TOM. The question said spouses!! Come on!! It's not some unplanned pregnancy!! You have the kid. You can't roll the dice and choose later. That's not... there's no integrity in that.
BART. Thank you Pope Tom.
ASHLEY. Jess, what about you?
JESSICA. Probably have the abortion.

TOM. *(Shocked.)* How can you say that? We've had this discussion.

JESSICA. The more I think about it though, the more I think it would be unfair to put somebody through that.

TOM. *(Smiling.)* This is ridiculous!! Two seconds ago you two were celebrating "The Body Shop" for defending the rights of a little beady eyed rat. So, basically, you want little cute Mr. Mousey to live free of persecution from men in lab coats, but you're telling me that a three month old baby should be discarded if defected.

JESSICA. I didn't say that.

STEPH. Fetus, Tom, not baby.

TOM. Fetus shmetus, it's a baby.

STEPH. No, it's not a baby until it's born. You can't even compare it with animal rights! It's one thing to end the life of a helpless animal that has no ability to defend itself against man's quest for a better after shave—

TOM. Or a better baby.

STEPH. No. A baby can't survive without parents. Animals survive without human intervention. Abortion is nothing more than ridding the body of an unwelcome parasite.

BOB/TOM/ASHLEY. Parasite!!??

STEPH. There is no life for a fetus without a woman!! Therefore she should be able to determine whether or not she wants it. It's a classic parasite/host relationship.

ASHLEY. Parasite... That's kind of disgusting.

STEPH. Only because society's defined parasite for you. It's not necessarily a disgusting thing. It's a factual thing.

TOM. Unbelievable.

ASHLEY. Bart?

BART. No way. Too much work.

TOM. What?

BART. Hey, I'm telling the truth.

TOM. You're pathetic.

ASHLEY. Bob?

BOB. Never getting married dude, so I don't know which spouse I'd be conferring with. Looks like I'm out of the question.

STEPH. *(Grabbing the book.)* New question!

TOM. Can we can the questions? I wanna make an announce—

STEPH. C'mon! We're stirring things up. Good for the blood. If you were in a long term relationship with someone who wasn't sexually satisfying to you, would you tell them?

TOM. Definitely.

BART. Of course.

BOB. I usually pass out before I have time to reflect on it.

ASHLEY. Well, most men don't know where or how to touch a woman.

BART. Ashley!

JESSICA. I agree.

TOM. Hold on, maybe some men don't, but the ones who ask never have a problem, and anyway, who's fault is it if a man doesn't know how to specifically turn on a certain woman?

ASHLEY. Fault?

TOM. Yeah, you both make these snide comments as if all women are turned on the same way. Proper loving men search out the personal ground.

BOB. It's instinct dude.

JESSICA. Oh Bob, enough of your rock-star-lover-god impersonation. You seem to forget that I roomed with your girlfriend junior year. Know what she called you? Three minute Bob.

(Everyone but BOB, laughs.)

BART. Bob unplugged!!!!
BOB. Least I got mine.
STEPH. See, that's the sort of selfish attitude too many men have!! "Least I got mine." That's a heroic comeback! See, most men don't know how to really get a woman aroused because they're too busy getting off on how cool and macho they think they look performing the act. Don't you agree?
ASHLEY. That's been my experience.
BART. Ashley!!!!!
TOM. Can we stop this? Are we going to visit and hang out or are we going to argue all night?
JESSICA. We're not arguing, we're discussing, stirring it up!
TOM. Well, the blood we're stirring up in this discussion is about to give Bart an aneurysm.
JESSICA. If people get riled up, let them. What are you, a wimp?
TOM. What?
JESSICA. What is it Tom? Are you afraid to truthfully examine and take on topics that explore the divisions between the sexes?
TOM. No, Jess, I just don't want to get into this.
JESSICA. You men are all the same. Cowards.
TOM. What?
JESSICA. You heard me. All men, deep down, are cowards.
TOM. Cowards of what?

JESSICA. The truth. For one. Reality. Two. The real world. Three.

TOM. What is it with these sweeping generalizations? Look Jess, don't preach to me abut what you've conjured up in your mind as the truth. I'm a compassionate, liberal man... trying to live out equality, human rights, etc., it's just not vogue to accept that coming from a young middle class male.

JESSICA. And it's about time!!!! Look at you, you're coming from a point of view where you're not even able to experience any inequality or discrimination, so how could you even begin to understand it?

TOM. Oh my God--How did we get into this?

JESSICA. Come volunteer with me at the girls home one Saturday afternoon when you're not watching football and scarfing back potato chips. Come along with me to get an idea of cowardly men and their victims. That's right, victims. Teenage girls having babies strung out on crack. Babies that haven't a chance in hell of surviving, but these girls don't even think of abortions. Why? Because they want someone to love. To hold. Because deadbeat men, overgrown boys, ditch them. It's sickening. Admit it.

BART. Look guys—

JESSICA. *(Combative.)* Can you fucking admit it?

TOM. What does this have to do with anything?!! You're going off Jess, calm down!

JESSICA. Why don't you calm down? You're afraid to admit I'm right and you're wrong.

TOM. I'm not afraid--I just don't want to argue.

JESSICA. Who's arguing?

TOM. Okay slow down. Honey, I'm sorry—

JESSICA. Don't start patronizing me!
TOM. I'm not patronizing you!!
JESSICA. Don't touch me! (*Tom throws his hands up and turns away.*) Oh okay walk away!! Walk away!!! Don't confront your life. Just walk away! Well fuck you, I'm leaving!

(She exits, slamming the door.)

TOM. What just happened?
ASHLEY. Tom, she's been stressing about a lot of things lately. Don't take it personally. Stay here--I'll... I'll go catch up with her.
TOM. Yeah.
BOB. *(Moving towards TOM, trying to console him.)* It'll be alright. Let's chow dude.

(Lights down.)

Scene 5

(Lights up on ASHLEY and JESSICA, at their apartment. JESSICA is packing.)

ASHLEY. Well...
JESSICA. Well what?
ASHLEY. I think...
JESSICA. What?
ASHLEY. This...
JESSICA. This what?
ASHLEY. This outpouring--is a symbol.

JESSICA. Wha'--What is that supposed to mean?
ASHLEY. You know...
JESSICA. I do not.
ASHLEY. You do.
JESSICA. I do not "know" Ashley.
ASHLEY. Well, don't you think it's part of your pattern, kind of?
JESSICA. Pattern?!! I do not have a pattern!
ASHLEY. You kinda do Jess. It sounds to me like you're making it fit this opportunity to move to New York with Stephanie.
JESSICA. This isn't about Stephanie. Look, I don't want to wake up at forty-five and have nothing to point to but a hunk of cellulite, and be some bitter woman with three kids, a fat ass, and an empty soul!! It's nobody's fault but my own, and nobody wants to hear some woman bitch about how she could have been a successful actress and just uh, I--My tank is empty. It's time to move on.
ASHLEY. To New York?
JESSICA. I owe it to myself to try Ashley. I can't stay here on this gerbil wheel spinning myself into insanity. Look at me! I feel like I've been on this track to some god awful place where I'll be burping babies and Tom'll be fat and bald and grilling kielbasa on our stainless steel gas barbecue, and we'll rake leaves together on Saturdays and like it, and shop at yard sales all weekend and like it, and go to "Friday's" and eat fake Cajun style food and like it, and my soul just screams out no!!!!!!! It's too soon to be shopping for tile samples at white stucco mini malls, you know?
ASHLEY. *(Pointing to a tape JESSICA has just packed.)* That's my Dead bootleg.

JESSICA. Oh. Sorry.

(Jessica unpacks the tape.)

ASHLEY. I think you should really rethink this.

JESSICA. You think I'm just "doing" this? Like I haven't thought about it? You're not hearing what I'm saying. You're judging me! And don't judge me just because you cling.

ASHLEY. Cling?

JESSICA. KA-LING.

ASHLEY. That is--That is such bullshit.

JESSICA. It is not. If you want to discuss patterns—

ASHLEY. What pattern!?

JESSICA. Denial.

ASHLEY. What!?

JESSICA. I face, you space.

ASHLEY. Oh, c'mon.

JESSICA. You don't know what you'd do if you weren't in a relationship.

ASHLEY. Hey, don't attack me just because I'm playing devil's advocate!!

JESSICA. Well, who's side are you on?

ASHLEY. Who said I had to pick sides? This affects a lot of us.

JESSICA. *(Beginning to lose her cool.)* Oh... now I have to be concerned about how it's going to affect all of us. Is this another pattern Ashley? Is this my "not thinking of how my breakup will affect my friends-syndrome?" See!!!... My only identity is part of a couple known as Jess/Tom. We do the same things with the same people and we call each other good friends yet we gossip about each other and judge each other and back stab and know way too much about each other. *(Angry.)* Is that the definition of Friendship? Our lives are so intertwined it's suffocating! I can't not do something because my friends may think I'm-- *(Realizing she's losing it.)* ...Oh the hell with it. I talk too much.

ASHLEY. Look, you may have a lot of things on your mind, you may be frustrated, you may feel like your life is speeding past you, but hell Jess, everybody feels that fifty percent of the time—

JESSICA. I feel that way all the time.

ASHLEY. Then go see somebody and get if off your chest! But you've got to deal without tearing into your friends. When did you adopt this attitude about your friends being backstabbing losers you're forced to be around? What is going on with you? I care about you. You are my best friend. The truth of it, is that if you and Tom break up, it will affect all of us. Our lives will change. There'll be a gap, and you know... we won't be able to do the same things with both of you.

JESSICA. What the... I don't know... I'm so lost. What am I going to do?

ASHLEY. All I'm trying to say is, you can work this out. You guys have a lot to lose if you walk away. He'd move for you. I mean, you still love him, right? Just talk to him.

JESSICA. Yeah. Yeah.

(Lights down.)

Scene 6

(An hour later. Lights up on TOM entering JESSICA'S apart-

ment. ASHLEY has left.)

JESSICA. Tom, we should talk.

TOM. *(As he removes his coat.)* Look, I'm sorry if I was being insensitive or macho, or anti-woman back there... I, I, I'm sorry. I guess I was just kinda on edge tonight. I just don't think sometimes and I joke at the —

JESSICA. No, I'm sorry for the way I acted back there. There's no excuse for that. I'm sorry.

TOM. Well, good, I'm glad we've made up, because there was something I was going to ask—

JESSICA. Tom, I don't know, have you sensed any weird vibes you know, lately?

TOM. Well, if slammed doors count as vibes—

JESSICA. I've had a lot on my mind lately.

TOM. I could tell by—

JESSICA. Tom, I really care for you.

TOM. What's bothering you? You can tell me.

JESSICA. This is hard.

TOM. What?

JESSICA. Things aren't working.

TOM. What?

JESSICA. Things have changed.

TOM. Hold on a second, we got into an argument, Jess, and I said I'm sorry—

JESSICA. I need to be on my own for a while.

TOM. What are you talking about—

JESSICA. This isn't working.

TOM. Jess, hold on, you're talking crazy here, we got in a little argument.

JESSICA. No, Tom, we've been growing apart.

TOM. When?

JESSICA. My heart is telling me it's time for a change so—

TOM. WAIT A MINUTE, SLOW DOWN!! Who are you talking to? "My heart is telling me," what? What?

JESSICA. I'm moving to New York!

TOM. What!!?

JESSICA. I've got to give this acting thing a shot.

TOM. Acting, this about acting!!?

JESSICA. No it's about hiding!! I'm hiding from my reality! I'm wrapped up in some dream that I'll be discovered walking down Newbury street or as an extra in some third rate independent horror film here in Boston, but in reality--I've given up!!

TOM. You've got an acting job now!!

JESSICA. No, Tom, I'm a beer wench at the "Medieval Manor." I serve beer to drunk plumbers from Revere. I sing an occasional ballad from the middle ages that no one listens to. It's not acting!! *(Beat.)* I've really fulfilled my potential!

TOM. Let's take it down a notch for a second here. This is completely crazy! Talk some sense here! First of all, if you were going to move to New York, where would you even live?

JESSICA. With Stephanie.

TOM. You're kidding me.

JESSICA. What!?

TOM. Nothing. I'm sure you'll love living with feminism's new Yoda.

JESSICA. Tom, you don't have to bad mouth my friend—

TOM. Oh yeah, your friend. How many times have you talked to her in the past year? She stops in on the way to her parents' house, she leaves you an occasional message on your voice mail, and you catch her at a wedding for a mutual friend every, what? twenty-nine months? That's a real blood sister you have working there.

JESSICA. She's letting me live in her apartment for free! And so what if she's changed?! I never thought you, of all people, would be against change.

TOM. I'm against Stephanie, who's not even in touch with your life right now, coming in here and preaching some paperback pop psychology sermon to the woman I love and who I want to spend the rest—

JESSICA. I've decided this Tom!! It's not about some sermon or somebody else! It's not about Stephanie. It's about me!

TOM. But don't you see? Then it's about me too.

(TOM pauses as JESSICA says nothing. He tries to regain the momentum driven by his reason for being there: his proposal.)

TOM. There's something I want to say that I think will put things back in perspective.

(He feels for the ring in his pocket.)

TOM. I think we've both just had some crazy tough times... You know things--things haven't fallen into place in our careers exactly like we wanted but hey--you know, there's no certainty in life right?

JESSICA. Tom, you're not—

TOM. Let me finish. Please. There's no certainty in life— but there is, I believe, certainty in trust and in commitment. And a guy's life is worth nothing without a wonderful woman

to share it with. And this... what we have... this history, this relationship-type of thing doesn't come along everyday. I know 'cause I see other people and they don't have what we have. And Jessica, I love you. This is the real thing for real.
JESSICA. Tom...
TOM. I know you're frustrated with some things, but all in all, we can't let that get in the way of what--what we have. And I, I want the honor before God and family and my friends, of vowing to be your husband for life. I want to ask for the honor of your hand in marriage.

(He takes out the ring and presents it.)

    JESSICA. Oh, Tom.
    TOM. This is when you say "yes."
    JESSICA. Tom... I--I'm not ready to say "yes."

(For a second he is speechless. Stunned.)

    TOM. <u>Not ready</u>? Jessica, we've been together for six years!! How much more time do you need?
    JESSICA. Don't yell!
    TOM. *(Desperate.)* I'm sorry. Jess, this isn't a joke, I planned this, I met with your Dad and everything... I want to do this right, I want to do this... Jess, I--I'm ready to live a life with you. I want to be your husband!! I want you to raise a family with me!! I want to create a home, and a life, and walk side by side and hook arm and arm and be able to-- to point to you and tell people: "This is my wife!"
    JESSICA. I am not going to be ornamental decoration on a guy's life!

TOM. Ornamental dec-- What are you talking about? That's not the —

JESSICA. I am not moving to Rhode Island!!

TOM. Rhode Island? Okay! I thought—

JESSICA. What?

TOM. I--I can move to New York. They have schools there, right? Kids play soccer there, right?

JESSICA. Tom. Yes. Yes. *(Lays it on the line.)* Tom, it's not about you moving. I--I just can't settle down yet. I have to go alone. There's places I need to see if I can get to on my own.

TOM. I don't get it. This doesn't come along everyday! I don't get it. I don't understand why you didn't bring it up so we could talk about it. What is that?

JESSICA. I wasn't going to blurt out some random worries—

TOM. Random worries! It's our life together! It's six years!! You act like we're at some junior high school dinner dance and you're telling me we can't go out anymore because I'm not cool or something. This is outta nowhere!! Jessica, please talk to me! Why is this so etched in your mind? When did this become non-negotiable? This is crazy!! What about our thing? Me? This—

JESSICA. Tom, wait a second and let me—

TOM. Is there somebody else?

JESSICA. *(She's shocked, but says softly.)* Tom, no. No.

TOM. Then stop a second and think. Follow your heart and listen. How do you feel about me?

JESSICA. I'll always have a special place for you.

TOM. "A special place?" What, a little crawl space in the upper left had corner of your heart—

JESSICA. Tom!

TOM. ...a little cubby hole, a cozy nook next to the guy who took your virginity? "A special place!" A "place?" What do I want "a place" for? I had the whole goddamn thing!

JESSICA. You're not letting me—

TOM. *(Loudly.)* What?! You are a different person like that!! *(Snaps fingers.)* You are completely talking irrationally. You're crazy!! This is fucking psychotic!!!! What the hell—

JESSICA. I don't love you anymore!!

(This is a bullet to his heart. Silence.)

TOM. *(Stunned.)* What?

(It is harder to say a second time, but she must if she is to move on.)

JESSICA. I--I don't love you anymore.

(He is crushed. He has no words.)

JESSICA. Tom, I still care for you. About you. I do! This isn't easy for me! Don't you understand?

(She reaches for him, but he pulls away.)

TOM. *(Almost inaudibly.)* Don't touch me.

(He throws the ring to the floor, gathers his coat and exits slowly.)

JESSICA. Where are you going--Jesus!! I'm trying to be honest with you. Tom! Tom?!

(Lights down.)

END OF ACT I

ACT II

Scene 1

(One year later. TOM sits at a typewriter in his apartment. BOB enters through the front door.)

BOB. Hey Tom!
TOM. What's Up?
BOB. Uh. The sky. *(Laughs.)*
TOM. What?
BOB. What's with you?
TOM. Nothing. I--I've got to get this resume done.
BOB. You alright?
TOM. I'm fine. You alright?
BOB. You mad at me?
TOM. No.
BOB. Good.
TOM. *(To the typewriter.)* The hell with this.
BOB. Tom, what's up?
TOM. Nothing.
BOB. Get it off your chest.

(TOM is miffed as he holds up a letter he wrote to JESSICA.)

TOM. Can you believe she sent me back another letter unopened? Can you believe this?!!!
BOB. Oh. Tom... I don't know how many times I gotta tell you, but you're better than her.
TOM. Yeah well, she's Miss TV and I'm still working for

UPS. Which at this point stands for: U Piece of Shit.

BOB. Sometimes people gotta go through a real shitty relationship to find true love.

TOM *(Baffled.)* What?

BOB. Love's a tricky thing.

TOM. *(Sarcastic.)* Really Bob, tell me.

BOB. You just, you never know when it will hit you or shift or change or bloom.

TOM. Is this supposed to make me feel better?

BOB. I think certain loves are destined to be. You and Jess--it wasn't destiny.

TOM. What?!! Destiny?! I think destiny is a cop out for people scared of being held accountable for making a choice. Yeah. So they chalk it up to some astrological alignment or God plan.

BOB. It was just —

TOM. Don't say it!

BOB. What?

TOM. I know what you're going to say.

BOB. No you don't.

TOM. Then say it.

BOB. No.

TOM. Say it.

BOB. Relax.

TOM. I know what you were going to say.

BOB. No you don't. *(Beat.)* I was going to say that it's all in the—

TOM. Timing!! See! Timing!! Timing!!! "It's all in the timing!" "Your time wasn't right!" "You're moving in different orbits!" I'm sick of that as an explanation.

BOB. You just gotta find somebody new.

TOM. Somebody new?!! Bob! Look at you--first off, "somebody new"--like I meet a whole lotta new people around here! Gimme a break! I'm not going to date some twenty-one year old college girl that you sold some t-shirt to, so, what? I'm left with some woman I meet at some party or some tailgate at some football game some random friend throws? I mean do you have any idea how much emotional baggage comes with people by the time they hit their late twenties? Right off the bat you're getting a woman who's had her heart broken two or three times, maybe more--forget how many she's broken herself! And without a doubt she's had great sex with at the very least five guys--unless she's a prude--and if that's the case who the hell wants to deal with that at this point, you know? I mean "somebody new!" You know something? Regardless of how great you might get along with "Miss Somebody New," she's got a back up hard drive's worth of memorable experiences with other guys at ski lodges, summer houses, family outings, college parties, pictures of romantic embraces with these jackasses you don't even know! Not that you'd want to know them. I'm just saying, that's a hell of a lot of history to get by, you know? And what it all boils down to is that if I'm dating "somebody new" who knows where I'm going to be when some explosive memory is gonna be triggered that's gonna remind some new woman I'm dating of one of her old boyfriends? Come on! I mean what?! I'm gonna be out on a date and some woman's gonna break into tears just because some random Bruce Springsteen tune comes on!! I can just see it!! I'm sitting there eating some Buffalo wings thinking "Miss Somebody New " is digging me but she's really just remembering where she was, when she was with "boyfriend she thought she was gonna marry number three," and they were driving cross country four years ago gazing into each other's eyes when "Born to Run" came on the radio and so she's all misty eyed and aloof missing him, trying to explain to me why she's crying and I'm sitting across from her, sick to my stomach, unable to finish my wings or my nachos because I don't wanna hear her old boyfriend stories! I don't wanna know how much she loved somebody else once! I don't! Call me crazy! Call me nutso, call me a cab to goddamn Wackoland, but the fact is, I don't have time to fill a new photo album with "somebody new!" As far as I'm concerned, you can take all the "somebody news" in the whole goddamned world and you can blow them out your ass!! I liked my life with somebody old. I liked my history with Jessica. I liked what I had.

BOB. Uh-yeah dude. Whatever...

TOM. It's all a crock of shit anyways!

BOB. Why is everything a crock of shit to you nowadays?

TOM. Everything is. This resume. Look at me! Look at this apartment!! I'm working on a typewriter!! A fucking typewriter!!!!! I don't have a teaching job. I don't have a coaching job. Soccer coaching? What the hell do I know? "Kick the ball! Run!" Crock of shit. I'm going down to the pub.

BIB. Tom, it's three o'clock in the afternoon.

TOM. You're telling me when I can or can't get drunk?

BOB. No.

TOM. So... Later.

(TOM exits.)

BOB. Later.

(Lights down.)

THREE YEARS FROM "THIRTY" 61

Scene 2

(The same day. Lights up on Jessica at a coffee bar in New York City. She's on a blind date with Victor Spindle, a man in his late twenties.)

VICTOR. So, I've got to admit, I'm not a big fan of soap operas, but it is kinda cool being out with a star.

JESSICA. I'm not a star.

VICTOR. Getting mobbed at Tower Records means you're a star.

JESSICA. I wasn't mobbed.

VICTOR. Okay, well, four teenage girls were clamoring for your autograph. I'd call that a star. Stephanie told me you were an actress, not a star.

JESSICA. A familiar face.

VICTOR. This year's "new face!" With that buzz you'll soon be on the cover of "People" magazine.

JESSICA. Hold on. Hold on. I don't know. It's all happening so fast, I'm not so sure I want to be on the cover of "People." That'd be lowering my integrity as an artist in a way... exploiting, I don't know. What the hell am I talking about? I'm on a soap opera.

VICTOR. Exactly... for me--there are no rules. Integrity? Integrity is flexible. You hear people all the time: "I won't do this." "I won't do that." That's a big load of dog do. A verbal prison. Don't get me wrong. I'm not talking about you. Other people. What that is, is four walls of moralistic preachy cucka.

JESSICA. Pardon?

VICTOR. I'm not fooled by my psyche's pseudo longing for a moral higher ground. What is that? That is shit. More cucka! I look at what it is I want and I go for it.

JESSICA. But I think you—

VICTOR. May the means change... so be it. Loyalty? To who? A company? Bullshit, I give my company my precious life's clock ticking away and in return I get a salary. That's the system. That's the contract. Publishing? Bullshit. I get paid to listen to my boss unravel her sex life, her home life, and her visions of past lives, and if I continue to do that--I get incremental raises of a thousand dollars a year. That's it. Nothing deeper. Get the vibe? See, I've finally decided I'm making a life change. Because if I have to listen to somebody else's sex life, home life and half-lives, I want ten percent in return.

JESSICA. Where does fulfillment come in your plan?

VICTOR. Fill my wallet and I'll be fulfilled.

JESSICA. And when did you adopt this creed?

VICTOR. When I shed the myth.

JESSICA. Oh yeah, what myth was that?

VICTOR. The myth of commitment. Come on! Like these people, these higher ups, these mysterious corporate bosses, care about me? Like they're what--committed! Forget about it. Commitment. Triple dosage of cucka.

JESSICA. Stop using that word please.

VICTOR. Commitment?

JESSICA. No. Cu—

VICTOR. Cucka? It fits though, don't it? You've got to see through that cucka to get by. Get the vibe? Me, I've got to go for the gusto. Other people's values, they're like shackles man! I am not going to be fettered by the chains of some societal movement that screams out "Integrity!" "Commitment!" as if they're what? Doctrines of some dogmatic Utopia capable of being achieved in today's morass of civilization? Cu-uh-huh-uh-huh-huh-ka!! You'll just get boned in the end! Fuck it man. I'm getting mine.

JESSICA. You remind me of a guy I know.

VICTOR. Really? I bet I'm cuter. Heh-heh. But for his sake, I hope he's on the move. Cuz life is rolling by. Time to catch a rail or get steam rolled. I mean, jeez, look at me. I'm making 26.5 as an editorial assistant. I'm on a date in a yogurt shop/coffee bar/pastry joint. Now, I'm having a great time, but, it's time to make the move to own the fitness centers and yogurt shops.

JESSICA. By being a literary agent?

VICTOR. Are you kidding me? Yes. Literary agents are the very guts of the multimedia superhighway. And, fact is, I've already discovered the next Hemingway. He just hasn't hit yet because he's got that obscurity thing going. But once he breaks big and I put him on CD ROM and start pumping him into people's PC's, bingo! I'm sliding over the rainbow and into the pot of gold.

JESSICA. Aren't you afraid you'll lose who you really are in all this? And that maybe it's already starting? I mean, I know this is our first date, but Stephanie told me you were starting a band.

VICTOR. I was. That's over. See, my sound was new wave pop metal stuff. That's already on the way out.

JESSICA. Uh-huh.

VICTOR. I'm just adjusting my viewfinder to the changing tide. I mean, hey, you're a big TV star. What am I but some wannabe hi-tech high roller, right? See, I want the reins to my life's stagecoach in my hands! You already got yours. You try to do NYC on $14 grand after taxes. Get the vibe? I broke one mold to fit into a more affluent one.

JESSICA. You hope.
VICTOR. I know.
JESSICA. How's that?
VICTOR. Stars come and go, agents remain.
JESSICA. Please. This is nauseating. You--you act like it doesn't come without a sacrifice. That it's easy.
VICTOR. Look at you. You moved here a year ago, you're a soap star.
JESSICA. I'm not a star.
VICTOR. You get paid to be on TV five days a week.
JESSICA. It's not what people think.
VICTOR. I didn't say it was perfect. You're on the right track by dating me though. Look. I just want to be more comfortable.
JESSICA. Be careful of what you lose in the process.
VICTOR. What? My dental plan? Forget about it. I lose the cross of security dressed up as a job in publishing that I've been bearing since college. I lose my go-nowhere career as an assistant to a peddler of nonfiction self help books to lost housewives, and long distance telephone salesmen looking for an "edge." I lose the shackles--I gain the light. I lose the chains, the wind is at my back, I thrust forward, start anew, embolden artists, encourage creativity, and all the while turn a profit.
JESSICA. Turn a profit? Is that your motto?
VICTOR. "Flexibility unbound" is my motto.
JESSICA. That's pathetic.
VICTOR. No, no. Kinetic. The motion's moving. I can't be stopped. The integrity will be returned once I have the power. I'm making a life change. And all this talking has me primed for another cup of Joe. You?
JESSICA. Ah... No. No, I think—

VICTOR. Come on. Live on the edge--Espresso.
JESSICA. No. I think I'm going to go home.
VICTOR. Well, I had a great time. It was great listening to you. I think we had a really feisty rapport, a nice thing, a good vibe, you know?
JESSICA. A vibe?
VICTOR. A vibe. Yeah. A good vibration here.
JESSICA. A vibe. Listen. There was no vibe. No "thing." No rapport. This date--you know what this date was? It was cucka! A big load of cucka! Okay?
VICTOR. Okay.
JESSICA. Let's leave it at that and cut our losses. I'm leaving now.

(She exits.)

VICTOR. Come on! I'll buy this round!

(Lights down.)

Scene 3

(Later the same day. Lights up on TOM in his apartment watching TV. He has the control in his hand and we hear JESSICA'S voice on the TV. In the midst of this, the door opens and BART enters, carrying a garment bag.)

BART. Tommy! Yo. What's doin'?
TOM. Nothing. You're home early.
BART. Yeah, tomorrow's meeting got canceled. I tell you,

I am sick of traveling. What are you watching--the game? I heard the Pats are gettin' their ass kicked again. What's the score?

    TOM. Think she's dating this actor guy?

    BART. Tom—

    TOM. Seriously.

    BART. Tom.

    TOM. If she's sleeping with that dippity do mole faced A-hole... Look at him!!

    BART. Buddy...

    TOM. *(To the television.)* Oh yeah, take your shirt off again loser, she really wants you, yeah right. *(To BART.)* He's taken his shirt off three times this episode.

    BART. When are you gonna stop with this?

    TOM. Lay off.

    BART. You gotta lay off Tom. You gotta lay off. Look at you man. You're watching videotapes of her shit ass soap opera! It's been a year!! A whole year! It's over!! *(Goes to a big box containing videotapes.)* It's time to get rid of these videotapes. Get rid of her.

    TOM. Put those down.

    BART. Tom, look at you man. This--this is eating--it's eaten you up. You're letting her get the best of you.

    TOM. I gave her the best of me.

    BART. Take it back!! Just because she left you, doesn't mean she gets to keep the best things about you when she leaves. You can move on without her. Think about it. You can. I know you can man. There's others out there.

    TOM. Not like her.

    BART. All the better.

    TOM. She was—

BART. Tom! She left you high and dry, hard and fast. Don't give her that. Don't cut her that slack. Forget her.

TOM. I just...

BART. What?

TOM. No one ever told me that falling in love meant surrendering yourself to the ebb and flow of someone else's tide.

BART. What the hell are you talking about? Where did you hear that miserable crap?

TOM. I read it.

BART. Where?

TOM. This card.

(He pulls out a greeting card that he's purchased for JESSICA'S birthday.)

BART. What? A Birthday card?!! For her? Did Bob get you high? Come on Tom!! Don't. Do not send it.

TOM. Her birthday's in two weeks.

BART. Fuck her birthday!! Gimme that!! *(He grabs the card.)* She is all your pain. Give birth to that and then get it out of your system like a big piece of shit you flush down the toilet. Enough is enough!! She left you! It's over and done with! I don't know why you're still so mired in this shit. You can't hold people to commitments Tom! People change their opinions like their bottled iced teas!! It's over Tom. It's been over. Pick yourself up. I gotta get you out of her. Let's go get some beers.

(He pulls TOM out of the chair and throws him a coat as they begin to exit.)

TOM. She looked pretty hot in that outfit though, huh?
BART. Move!

(They exit, and just as they do, BOB peeks out from the door of his bedroom. Seeing that the guys have gone, he walks out of his room. The phone rings. BOB picks it up.)

BOB. Hello. He's not here. Dude I can't find a pen. Yeah, Sean McCormick from Roxbury High. I got it. I'm sorry, Steve McCormick. Dude, I won't forget. *(As BOB looks for a pen, ASHLEY comes out from the bedroom.)* Okay. Cool. Yeah. I'll leave the message. I wrote it down. Later. *(He hangs up the phone without writing down the message and looks at the door.)* I thought you said he was out of town.

ASHLEY. He came back early! I thought you said Tom was out drinking!

BOB. He came back early. *(Beat.)* We gotta do something about this.

ASHLEY. I know, I know.

(They hug closely and softly.)

(Lights down.)

Scene 4

(Lights up on JESSICA and STEPHANIE in their New York City apartment. It's later, after JESSICA'S date with VICTOR.)

JESSICA. *(Walking in and dumping her backpack.)* Stop with these men, please.
STEPH. What?
JESSICA. "WHAT?" I'm just back from a blind date with the "creature from the coffee bar," your loser "friend" whose motto is "Integrity is flexible," that's what.
STEPH. Victor?
JESSICA. Yes Victor. Sick Vic. How do you meet these guys?
STEPH. His father's a doctor. I supply him with samples of Prozac.
JESSICA. Wonderful!
STEPH. Oh, don't worry, Victor's not on it. He's all toxin free.
JESSICA. I don't care if he's "Ollie ollie oxen free," I'm never going to see him again, so I don't care.
STEPH. Okay, so he's a little eccentric—
JESSICA. He's a pompous ass.
STEPH. Well, alright, so it didn't work out. It's probably a sign that somebody else is right around the corner. I mean hey, you're a big star. You can have the pick of the litter.
JESSICA. Stephanie. This is the fifth guy you've set me up with, and I've tried four on my own. I had my pick of the litter. Tom and I fit.
STEPH. Jess. Let's not get into this again. You made your move. You—
JESSICA. "Followed my bliss." I know.
STEPH. You can make it alone.
JESSICA. I have made it alone. Here I am. Wowee.
STEPH. Come on! You're up and coming! Off to the races!
JESSICA. Off to what race? Where? Against who? And

where do I end up?

STEPH. That's your choice babydoll.

JESSICA. I blew it.

STEPH. Stop talking like that.

JESSICA. I'm crazy. That's my problem. He loved me. I loved him. Why the hell couldn't I see—

STEPH. Jess--listen. I know the grieving is a necessary catharsis but—

JESSICA. Will you shut up?

STEPH. What?

JESSICA. Do you ever shut up?

STEPH. Are you talking to me like that? Or maybe yourself?

JESSICA. Can I just talk Stephanie? Can I just talk and you listen without an evaluation? I mean, I appreciate your concerns and we've been best friends forever, but can you for once let me finish a thought before you propel into some self actualization diatribe? I miss Tom. That's all.

STEPH. You're allowed to miss. I'll give you that. I just don't want you to beat yourself up about making a choice to leave--look what you've learned. You can't define yourself through the filter of a guy! You're making your dreams come true. You're living the dreams of thousands of people. Getting paid to act!!!

JESSICA. I just—

STEPH. What?

JESSICA. I'm—

STEPH. You know why you gotta get over this Jess. Because it kills you. You can't even speak.

JESSICA. You never realize what—

STEPH. "You've got till it's gone." Yeah, yeah. And you

also never know how great your future boyfriends are going to be, because you haven't met them yet. So there. Cheer up.

JESSICA. Did I tell you he went to see my—

STEPH. Father? Ah--this will be the sixtieth time I think. You're not gonna get over this till you forget him. I got over Mark, you'll get over Tom.

JESSICA. Steph, is this your version of getting over? Eating microwave popcorn on a Saturday night and watching a weepy movie on the VCR? Look at this--this facade of a complete life!! We've got our apartment with exposed brick and hardwood floors and we are living large! Come on! Give us a couple of pairs of stuffed animal slippers and kiss the future good-bye.

STEPH. Hey! I'm taking care of myself! And you are too, Jessica, and you can't forget all of that just because you had a bad date.

JESSICA. I had a miserable date Stephanie! How many more miserable dates can one person have? It's not that easy to find somebody new, you know? It's a minefield of losers out there!!

STEPH. And Tom's a big winner. Mr. "Sign here please!"

JESSICA. He needed the benefits! Tom was decent and loyal and kind. That goes a long way when it comes to kids.

STEPH. Time out! I'm sorry for interrupting again, but I, as your friend, am not going to let a little menstrual blood flow cause a brain logic hemorrhage here! Don't go getting freaky on me and start in with this old maid biological clock psychosomatic crap Jessica! You're throwing a pity party for yourself. You are on the brink of major success where you can have the powers and clout to dictate how you're treated.

JESSICA. I'm on a soap opera.

STEPH. Slow down and enjoy it for a while.
JESSICA. Almost a year.
STEPH. What?
JESSICA. Since Tom and I split.
STEPH. Best year of your life.
JESSICA. Night of my birthday.
STEPH. *(Seeing an opportunity to change the subject.)* That's right. Your birthday's in two weeks! Let's celebrate! What do you want to do?

(Beat.)

JESSICA. I think I'm going home. My parents are having a party for me, and they want me to go home... I got a couple of days off early next week anyway.
STEPH. Maybe we can rent a car and I'll take it to the Cape after I drop you off.
JESSICA. I'll probably fly.
STEPH. Oh so you are a star.
JESSICA. Sometimes.

(They both smile, but a look of concern is registered on JESSICA'S face.)

(Lights down)

Scene 5

(Lights come up on BOB and ASHLEY tiptoeing across the floor of TOM'S apartment. They stand at the door for a

moment and kiss as TOM opens the door to his bedroom, catching the tail end of the kiss. BOB shuts the door and turns to find TOM standing and staring at him.)

TOM. Bob, what's up?
BOB. *(Startled.)* Nothing. What's up with you? You feeling alright?
TOM. Bob, what's up?
BOB. I just told you. Nothing. Just hanging. I'm hung man. How 'bout you?
TOM. That was Ashley.
BOB. Who, that?
TOM. Yeah that.
BOB. Yeah, she left her purse here or something.
TOM. Really.

(Suddenly the door opens and Ashley enters without seeing TOM.)

BOB. Oh, hey Ash.
ASHLEY. I just had to kiss you one more time. *(She sees TOM and tries to cover.)* Hey Tom how ya doin'?
TOM. Good.
ASHLEY. Great. Okay. Well. Okay. Bye.
BOB. Okay bye.
TOM. Bye.

(She exits.)

BOB. *(Looking at TOM.)* What?

(TOM shakes his head.)

BOB. What?

TOM. What?! Bob! That's Bart's girlfriend!!

BOB. Not anymore.

TOM. What?

BOB. She's bookin on him.

TOM. What? What the hell is going on here? When?

BOB. Soon.

TOM. What are you going to say to Bart?

BOB. I'm not. He's not my boyfriend!

TOM. Hey dirtbag, in case you need a reminder, he's your friend!

BOB. No, Tom, he's your friend. He's my roommate.

TOM. *(Sarcastic.)* Good Bob, you're rationalizing.

BOB. Oh like you're the king of relationships. Cuddled up with old photo albums and videotapes.

TOM. Don't attack me because your guilt is setting in!! Sorry if I'm bursting your bubble of wonder love, dude.

BOB. Look. Bart checked out of his thing with Ashley a long time ago. He treats her like shit, he's always away and frankly, she's over it. That's the main reason I went with it. In her mind she'd already broken up with him.

TOM. I don't get it.

BOB. There's nothing to get. We love each other. We can't deny the feelings! You don't choose the people you fall in love with. It just happens.

TOM. Love? Is that what you two have Bob? Love? Yeah.

BOB. What we have is deep. It's real. For the first time in my life I've got somebody who just loves me for real. It's awesome. We're into the same things. You and your crocks of shit? We're not into this crock of shit life that people believe in man. She doesn't mock out my music or my lifestyle or my dreams. *(Beat.)* Hey, listen. I know it's gonna be a beat thing for Bart to handle at first. But that'll pass. Time heals, you know? Tom, she wasn't going to stay with him. And anyways, what's worse? A few moments of discomfort or misery for eternity? And you know something Tom? In the end I don't give a shit what you or anybody else thinks. I don't have to spend the rest of my life with you.

TOM. And all's fair in love and war, right? *(Beat.)* When did all this happen? This is "The guys," Bob. "The guys." You're gonna have to face him. He's coming back tonight you know.

BOB. I'll be outta here by then.

TOM. Outta here?

BOB. I was going to tell you next week, but... here's my next two months rent. It should cover you till you find somebody else. We've got some cash together, some T-shirts, we're bookin to "Dances with Wolves" country. I told you guys I'd get there. And Tom, listen, she's just going to say she's bailin'. She's not gonna tell him about us. So, dude, don't say nothin' and he'll never know about this part, okay? Don't make this more beat than it has to be. Sorry Tom, but, I'm outta here. Oh, I almost forgot, the other day this guy—

(He is cut off as the front door is thrown open and BART storms into the room. TOM stands between the other two men.)

BART. Where the fuck is Judas?!

BOB. Uh, listen Bart—

BART. Listen to what, a low life scumbag telling me—

BOB. I had to—

BART. Had to what, fuck my girlfriend? What? Tell me

you had to—
BOB. It just happened!
BART. C'mon Bob! You can be a little more inspired than that, can't you? She just broke down wailing like a five year old on the street five minutes ago. Surely you can also dredge up a little more emotion, can't you? You're gonna tell me that you just happened to fall into bed with my girlfriend and just happened to get all her clothes off and just happened to fuck her?
BOB. Look Dude, I'm sorry.
BART. Stick your dude lingo up your ass. Dick in the mouth.
BOB. Dude, I...
BART. Stop with the dude bullshit dude. I'm not your dude, okay cowboy? I want you to tell me straight. Say it for me... "I fucked your girlfriend." I just wanna be sure. Say it! Say it!
BOB. Dude, come on man...
BART. Come on, say it you prick! Say it!!!
BOB. No.

(BART spits in BOB'S face; BOB flies into him but TOM holds him back.)

BOB. Lemme go Tom, I've sucked up enough to this pompous asshole!!
BART. Yeah Tom! Let him go! He's really got a great reason to beat me up. A great excuse. Can't you hear him telling people? "I fucked his girl then kicked his ass!" What a real big man! You're the lowest of lows man... You're a leech; a lazy, no talent leech with nothing on your mind but smokin' dope and satisfying your animal instincts of eating, shitting, and fucking.

BOB. Not a bad life dude. Maybe if you thought that way you'd be where I am now.

(BART flies at BOB and TOM tries to restrain them both, but BOB throws BART to the ground. BART hits the floor and stays down, as he grabs his shoulder.)

BART. *(Pulling himself to his feet, as he holds his shoulder.)* You're scum... I've known you nine years man... You've betrayed me and you've lost your soul in the process pal... and the sorry thing is you don't even know it. *(Beat.)* You can have her... I don't give a shit. I've got better things to do.

(He exits.)

TOM. What is with you?
BOB. It's beyond my control.
TOM. Why do you have to be such a dick? We were all friends man.
BOB. You think I'm a dick. Fine. *(Beat.)* But how can you judge me for going after what you've lost? You sit around here pissed off and bitter because you don't have any love in your life. Well, that's how I felt for my whole life. So I'm not passing it by. You saw how Bart treated her. He didn't love her! And I thank God I finally woke up and realized how special she was!! Maybe this was in some twisted way, a gift to him. I mean, better an ex-girlfriend at 27 than an ex-wife at 34. You know? Time will heal, you know?
TOM. No, I don't know.

(TOM exits.)

(Lights down)

Scene 6

(The next night. BART is at the couch packing belongings.)

TOM. Hey guy... what's... what's going on?
BART. What's up?
TOM. Where have you been?
BART. I've been fine.
TOM. Yeah... I... was worried about you when you didn't come home last night.
BART. I'm fine.
TOM. Where's this week's trip?
BART. Back home.
TOM. Back home? To Minneapolis? That's cool.
BART. Cooler than school.
TOM. For how long?
BART. Indefinitely.
TOM. What do you mean?
BART. I mean it's not definite.
TOM. Oh. Alright. You take a leave of absence?
BART. Yeah. Kind of. They kind of gave me one.
TOM. *(Shocked.)* What do you mean? I thought you've been kicking ass!
BART. I've been kicked in the ass. Laid off Tom. They say shit comes in threes. I can't wait for my number three.
TOM. What happened?
BART. What do you think happened Tom? Read the newspapers. It's called downsizing.

TOM. But I thought the training program meant...

BART. It don't mean shit. Haven't you figured that out by now?

TOM. Temporary setback. You'll land on your feet.

BART. To what? To where?

TOM. Don't get down, man. You'll get your resume out there and have a job in no time.

BART. Where? Here? No. I'm not getting down, I'm getting real.

TOM. Don't head home. Stick here man. Things'll turn around. Look buddy, I'm sorry. Seriously, I'm really sorry about how things, have come about, but... C'mon man! Cheer up, we're both single. All those good times we had in the past... we can still have those! Take your own advice. Forget it! We'll gig like college days! Like the past!

BART. The past? I'm sick of my past. College?!! No offense, but the frat guy buddy thing just doesn't do it for me anymore. You know, look at me and Bob. The purpose of that friendship was completely exhausted somewhere around the last time we tapped a keg together. Did we admit it? No... because of some stupid "Big Chill" reunion that dances in all of our heads, we hold onto friendships which have no reason to be continued, except for the vision of some eight by ten framed group photo of all of us around a barbecue when we're all forty. I used to think "Wow, it would be so great to get together with a bunch of old college friends in a big old house and celebrate, reminisce, be older and be psyched we stayed in touch." But here I am, three years from thirty, and the last thing I want to be doing now, or ten years from now, is playing touch football and dancing around a kitchen table with Bob, Ashley, and everyone else, as we wrap leftover turkey burgers to a bunch of shitty songs. Pathetic. The hell with Bob and Ashley. They can go live their soulmate bullshit. I'm not waiting for Ashley to come back. I've seen what waiting for Jessica's done to you. *(Beat.)* Look, I gotta be getting—

TOM. You're outta here huh? Boom. Like that.

BART. Time to burn some bridges. Not you Tom. But some --you know. Listen I left two months rent on the refrigerator, it should cover you. Gimme a call; the other stuff I'm gonna send somebody to get next week. It's all packed up in my room.

TOM. Okay man.

BART. Hey, take care.

TOM. Yeah. This is so sudden. I can't believe all this—

BART. Tell me about it.

TOM. I'm bummed you're outta here man, no convincing you to stay?

BART. Movin' on Tom.

TOM. Okay. Call me if you, you know, wanna rap about anything, you know...

BART. Yeah, yeah I will. Oh well. Later Tom. Chin up. Bottom line: nobody has a handbook on this piece of shit called life so quit looking for one. Look, I'll see ya. Later.

TOM. Yeah, well safe trip, um, later.

(They hug quickly. BART exits, and TOM stands alone as he closes the door.)

(Lights down)

Scene 7

(Tom enters through the front door as the phone rings. He leaves the door open and rushes to the phone.)

TOM. Hello. This is Tom. Yes. Hi Steve. *(Beat.)* Yeah--from--from--from--yeah Roxbury High--I'm sorry, that was a long time ago and I'm--I'm good. How are you? What's going--what are you talking about? No I didn't get the message... I'm sorry. What?! No. Of course I--Lemme think--Yeah that sounds good. Sure we can talk--I'll come by tomorrow. That's great. I know the address, sure. I tell you Mr. McCormick-- Steve, we had that interview so long ago, I thought you'd forgotten--right. We'll talk then. Thanks! This is great! Bye.

(He hangs up the phone and finds JESSICA standing in the open doorway.)

TOM. Wha--... Hi.
JESSICA. Hi.
TOM. Uh--Um--Wow. Hi.
JESSICA. Hi—
TOM. What are you—
JESSICA. Can I—
TOM. Come in! Come in! I'm sorry.
JESSICA. *(She enters.)* Surprise.
TOM. Heh. Yeah. Yeah. Ah--wow--this place is a total mess. Not that that's unexpected.
JESSICA. Some things never change.

(Tom moves to cover up the videotapes by throwing his coat over them.)

JESSICA. What's that?
TOM. What? Oh these. Game tapes.
JESSICA. Game tapes?
TOM. Yeah, yeah we videotape the kid's soccer games, take notes on 'em... coach type of stuff.
JESSICA. You got a coaching job?
TOM. It's just a city league team.
JESSICA. Oh. You look good.
TOM. I look like shit. I've got a gut and I'm going bald.
JESSICA. You are not. Your hair looks fine. I mean full!! You do look great.
TOM. So what's up? I mean what's--why—
JESSICA. My parents are having a little celebration for my birthday.
TOM. Oh yeah! Happy birthday! Twenty...?
JESSICA. Eight.
TOM. Wow. Gettin' old.
JESSICA. So, I've been working so much I finally got a chance to come home and celebrate my birthday and the last year.
TOM. Great.
JESSICA. I can't believe it's been a year. It went by so fast.
TOM. Yeah. Turbo year. It just rocketed by.
JESSICA. Yeah. It's been hard to get home with work and promotional stuff. You know, for "Love and Neighbors."
TOM. What's that? A new musical?
JESSICA. No. It's a soap. Opera. A soap opera. You haven't seen it?

TOM. No.
JESSICA. Oh.
TOM. Oh, wait... that's--Ashley said--Is that on during the day?
JESSICA. Yes.
TOM. Oh yeah. Yeah. New soap opera.
JESSICA. Yes.
TOM. Yeah. No, I haven't seen it. But Ashley told me something one time in passing... Congratulations. Good for you. Wow. You happy?
JESSICA. Yes. Great pay. Exposure's great. I mean, I'm just starting to get used to it. I'm acting. But, you know, I walked right into this huge part right away.
TOM. Let me know when it's on and I'll tape it sometime.
JESSICA. I will.
TOM. Yeah, I'll check it out.
JESSICA. It's nothing great, but you know, a lot of people did soaps then movies.

(The next two lines are spoken at the same time.)

TOM. Why are you here?
JESSICA. I don't know why I'm here.
TOM. Talk.
JESSICA. *(Softening.)* Tom, I don't... there's no party. There's no "thing" at my folks house... I just... I've been thinking about this--I think of nothing else and maybe I was too proud and I needed to--. I miss you so much. I miss that you know me. I miss us.
TOM. Really? Is that why you sent back my letters unopened?
JESSICA. Tom, I'm sorry. I know that--I know that was

mean. It was really mean. I was trying to be... I needed. I knew I still loved you and I needed to get me on track--and if I didn't I would have fallen right back to you.

TOM. You said you didn't love—

JESSICA. I know what I said. I--God I don't know what the hell--I made myself feel that I had to do that... because my twisted head had me thinking I had to convince myself of it in order to make a break. Don't you understand?

TOM. No.

JESSICA. God, I sound like I'm complaining about this pathetic "Dream" but, it--I couldn't get married because it was the next thing to do. Then all I'd be left with was what I had done. Which up to last year was nothing.

TOM. You created a relationship!! That's not nothing.

JESSICA. I know that now. God knows I know that! I just --I miss you.

TOM. I miss you too.

(They reach for each other, but suddenly TOM pulls away.)

TOM. What am I doing? What am I--I'm not going to do this to myself.

JESSICA. I want to try and get back to—

TOM. Don't! What the--? What are you doing? Are you crazy?

JESSICA. Can't we start again?

TOM. From where?

JESSICA. From the beginning?

TOM. We're different people.

JESSICA. Older people. Better.

TOM. Older? Yes. Jaded? Definitely. Better? I don't know

THREE YEARS TO "THIRTY"

where better comes in--hopefully at making decisions.

JESSICA. Let me help you. Please just give me a chance to get through to you.

TOM. You walked right through me!

JESSICA. I had to!

TOM. Oh come on!!

JESSICA. What?!!

TOM. I had to?!! Had to?! Please. Go ahead. Let's hear it again.

JESSICA. Hear what?

TOM. Your "I had to find myself but I made a mistake in losing you speech."

JESSICA. Is that how you view this? That this is some speech I cooked up, waltzing in here with some I-made-a-mistake-climactic monologue? You're, you're wr-- you're right! In one sense. I made a mistake coming back here. *(She picks up her stuff and turns to exit.)* If this is how I—

TOM. You bailed!! On me!! On us!!

JESSICA. *(Turning back.)* I'm admitting I fucked up! What else do you want me to say Tom? To do? I know I bailed! I know I folded! I am not proud of this! I'm trying to find my way back. But I'm here now and I came back hoping there'd be a glimpse of something, of love, of passion, what we felt, to build again!!!

TOM. Are you fucking kidding me?

JESSICA. I'm leaving.

TOM. What else is new?

JESSICA. Tom, my life hasn't always been crystal clear. Maybe it is for you--Is there a stronger word for "Sorry?" Because I'll say it a thousand times! I've struggled over this Tom! Pride? Reason? Love? I can't make sense of it anymore.

I just--I thought I'd try. Look, I'm sorry if I hurt you.
    TOM. *(Saying with her.)* "Sorry if I hurt you." Spare us both.
    JESSICA. What's happened to you?
    TOM. Broken hearts lead to bitterness.
    JESSICA. I didn't mean—
    TOM. What?! What?! Jess, I've wanted to shake you, knock some sense into you for a year. You were my life! My future! When did you start thinking of our relationship as this barricade that was stopping you from achieving your goals? I don't--I've had so many things to ask, to say to you but I never got the chance.
    JESSICA. You're making up for it now.

    (There is an uncomfortable laugh between them. Then a beat before TOM continues.)

    TOM. *(Softly.)* My life's been a shambles.
    JESSICA. Tom... I don't know how to start again, but I just know, I'm better. I feel like I'm in the right place... like I've finally accomplished something... and I thought that you could come to NYC, I'm making money, I've got a great job, I'm on the right track finally. I just got a little tripped up--a lot tripped up--but now, it's like I'm, I don't know, except for you--almost whole—
    TOM. Almost whole? I'm not even close to whole! Look at me! I've become a legendary loser.
    JESSICA. *(Sweetly.)* You're not a loser. You're a winner. Remember? Big jackpot O'guy. We just got derailed. Detoured. Come back to me. Be with me, Tom. Forgive me.

(Long beat.)

TOM. When you first left, I would crawl up into my bed and wrap my comforter around me, except, I'd scrunch up by the left side, because that was your side of the bed and it still smelled like you... your hair, your neck... I'd shut my eyes and just try to remember. Remember what it felt like, what your skin felt like. Every time I did that, I would come back to that time, we'd maybe been dating two months, when I woke up in the middle of the night and found you sitting up in bed wide awake. Remember? I rubbed my eyes and put my left hand on your right knee--you were sitting Indian style right next to me--And I said "Is everything okay?" And you said "I just like looking at you sleep." Then we both said "I love you," for the first time at the same time. Same time. That was so intense. I've had a hard time forgetting stuff like that. Some days I'd think I was fine. Then I'd walk around, and I'd see some guy eating his lunch and I'd remember the notes you'd hide in my sandwiches telling me I was your favorite friend. Or I'd put on some mixed tape you made me six summers ago, and I'd be a bag of shit for a week. *(Pointing to the tapes.)* Those are videotapes of your soap opera. I've seen it once or twice. Yeah. Love? A glimpse of love? I think of nothing else.

JESSICA. I know Tom. I know. It was real.

(Beat.)

TOM. It was as real as it gets. Which means, it should be a no-brainer, right? Because for a year I've been in a daze desperately hoping you'd walk through that door. And everything in my body wants to cling to you, grab hold, and jump a piggy back ride to wherever the hell you go next and figure it all out from there. But... I wouldn't be giving you anything remotely like the guy I used to be. Who used to be somebody you know.

JESSICA. No, Tom, I know you—

TOM. No, you've changed and I've changed, and everything's changing, everything's changed. This wasn't all your fault. I made plans without consulting you, I held you back, I didn't listen. I was so dead set on some hero man breadwinner bullshit that doesn't have any validity when two people and two lives and two hearts and two souls are trying to find parallel roads to carry their dreams together. And this year I've ripped apart my life, my friendships, my self-esteem and my dreams because I was so proud, so hung up on my own devastation. Diggin myself a pathetic self pitying ostrich hole, and... that's nobody's fault but my own.

JESSICA. Tom--I want—

TOM. I know what you want Jessica. I want the same thing. But the only thing I need more than being with you is being who I once thought I could be first. *(Beat.)* Two seconds ago I go a job offer at Roxbury High. It'll just be filling in for this woman on maternity leave but, listen, Jess, I'm not saying I don't understand what you needed to do, or understand people making mistakes, it's--I'm so much less than any guy I used to be, and I gotta stop feeling sorry for myself and get back to-- I've never given myself a first chance without you, and I've got—

JESSICA. What can I say to make it--Tom? I screwed up. I'm so sorry.

TOM. Me too. *(Beat.)* But I think you should go.

JESSICA. *(Stunned.)* Wha—

TOM. I think you should go.

(There's a long beat. She realizes he's serious.)

JESSICA. I've... I've... I'm going to... Yeah, I'm gonna...

(She opens the door and exits. TOM stands, staring at the door for a moment, and then closes it softly. Then he moves to the center of the room, sits down, sighs deeply and stares into his future, as the lights fade down to TOM, sitting alone.)

END OF PLAY

PROPERTY LIST

ACT I

Scene 1

UPS Uniform; shirt, pants, hat
UPS brown cardboard box
Daisy bouquet
Cellular Phone
Furniture - Coffee table, 2 chairs, couch
Six-pack of beer
Engagement ring
Cordless telephone
Vanity Fair magazine
Bong
Tobacco (marijuana substitute for bong)
Briefcase
Bottle of Jaegermeister
Three shot glasses
Stereo
Mail

Scene 2

Light beers of some sort
Salad materials
Book: "Care of the Soul"
Backpack for Stephanie
Glasses for beer

Scene 3
Alka-Seltzer
Advil
Coffee in paper cups
Newspaper

Scene 4
Pizza
Discarded pizza boxes
Twelve-packs of Rolling Rock beer
Assorted Birthday boxes for Jessica
Discarded wrapping paper
Soaps and stuff from "The Body Shop"
Book
Guitar for Bob

Scene 5
Bags for Jessica's clothing, etc.
Clothing for bags, etc.
Cassette tape for Grateful Dead bootleg

Scene 6
Engagement ring

ACT II

Scene 1
Typewriter
Paper
Letters for Jessica marked "Return to Sender"

Scene 2
Table and two chairs
Cups of coffee

Scene 3
Television
VCR
Box of Videotapes
Garment Bag
Greeting Card

Scene 4
Backpack
Microwave Popcorn

Scene 5
Check for Bob to give to Tom

Scene 6
Garment bag and belingings for Bart

Scene 7
Telephone
Blanket to cover Videotapes
Carrying bag for Jessica

Set Designer's Notes

The set for the original production of THREE YEARS FROM "THIRTY" was for the most part, extremely minimalist. Considering the production cost concerns, and the fact that our stage was too small for a revolving set, we needed to establish the idea of three apartments, a coffee shop, and an outdoor street, with a combination of lighting, and a few suggestive props. The principal setting that we used for our production is not in any way a "rule," of course, but merely a guide to be used in accordance with the needs of each production.

The principal setting should consist of a very generic brownstone-style, living room setting. This setting should not seem unique to one apartment, especially since it will be constantly switching between two Boston locales in Act I, and then changed to the New York living room in Act II.

The basic set should also include two doors upstage right and one downstage left. The doors can be used as bedroom entrances for one apartment, and then can be switched to act as a front door for the other apartment. The walls surrounding the doors should be a muted wainscoting paneling up to the half-wall level only.

In addition, the changes between the apartments can be executed through a variety of prop and set dressing changes executed by the actors. The idea is to keep it simple. We found that by covering the changes with contemporary music, the changes worked well. In order to avoid the chance that stagehands would be bumping into one another in the dark, we left the changes to the actors, and it worked magnificently.

There was no moving of the furniture, so the changes moved quickly.

To signify and symbolize the change in setting, the set changes can be a lay-out of extremes. Some examples which we found to be effective were sticking to stereotypes which drew a line of recognition for our audience. Following that thinking, we created two hanging wooden posters with beer advertisements and sports themes for the men's apartment, and a print of a famous painting or a black and white photograph print for the women's apartment. At the end of each scene, the exiting actors merely flipped the poster to its appropriate side and the transformation was nearly complete. To help that along, we included a ratty, coffee stained bedspread for the men's apartment and replaced it with a wonderful Native American knitted blanket when the women took over. The New York apartment had it's own set of hand props but the idea was the same. A poster of The New York skyline that was placed on-stage at intermission did the trick.

The scenes which take place outside of the apartment should be played in a small, downstage pool of light, and the actors should strike their props and, in the case of the coffee bar scene, their table and chairs, as they exit.

MURDER AMONG FRIENDS
Bob Barry

Comedy thriller / 4m, 2f / Interior

Take an aging, exceedingly vain actor; his very rich wife; a double dealing, double loving agent, plunk them down in an elegant New York duplex and add dialogue crackling with wit and laughs, and you have the basic elements for an evening of pure, sophisticated entertainment. Angela, the wife and Ted, the agent, are lovers and plan to murder Palmer, the actor, during a contrived robbery on New Year's Eve. But actor and agent are also lovers and have an identical plan to do in the wife. A murder occurs, but not one of the planned ones.

"Clever, amusing, and very surprising."
– *New York Times*

"A slick, sophisticated show that is modern and very funny."
– WABC TV

SAMUELFRENCH.COM

SKIN DEEP
Jon Lonoff

Comedy / 2m, 2f / Interior Unit Set

In *Skin Deep*, a large, lovable, lonely-heart, named Maureen Mulligan, gives romance one last shot on a blind-date with sweet awkward Joseph Spinelli; she's learned to pepper her speech with jokes to hide insecurities about her weight and appearance, while he's almost dangerously forthright, saying everything that comes to his mind. They both know they're perfect for each other, and in time they come to admit it.

They were set up on the date by Maureen's sister Sheila and her husband Squire, who are having problems of their own: Sheila undergoes a non-stop series of cosmetic surgeries to hang onto the attractive and much-desired Squire, who may or may not have long ago held designs on Maureen, who introduced him to Sheila. With Maureen particularly vulnerable to both hurting and being hurt, the time is ripe for all these unspoken issues to bubble to the surface.

"Warm-hearted comedy … the laughter was literally show-stopping. A winning play, with enough good-humored laughs and sentiment to keep you smiling from beginning to end."
– *TalkinBroadway.com*

"It's a little Paddy Chayefsky, a lot Neil Simon and a quick-witted, intelligent voyage into the not-so-tranquil seas of middle-aged love and dating. The dialogue is crackling and hilarious; the plot simple but well-turned; the characters endearing and quirky; and lurking beneath the merriment is so much heartache that you'll stand up and cheer when the unlikely couple makes it to the inevitable final clinch."
– *NYTheatreWorld.Com*

SAMUELFRENCH.COM

THE OFFICE PLAYS
Two full length plays by Adam Bock

THE RECEPTIONIST
Comedy / 2m, 2f / Interior

At the start of a typical day in the Northeast Office, Beverly deals effortlessly with ringing phones and her colleague's romantic troubles. But the appearance of a charming rep from the Central Office disrupts the friendly routine. And as the true nature of the company's business becomes apparent, The Receptionist raises disquieting, provocative questions about the consequences of complicity with evil.

"...Mr. Bock's poisoned Post-it note of a play."
– *New York Times*

"Bock's intense initial focus on the routine goes to the heart of *The Receptionist's* pointed, painfully timely allegory... elliptical, provocative play..."
– *Time Out New York*

THE THUGS
Comedy / 2m, 6f / Interior

The Obie Award winning dark comedy about work, thunder and the mysterious things that are happening on the 9th floor of a big law firm. When a group of temps try to discover the secrets that lurk in the hidden crevices of their workplace, they realize they would rather believe in gossip and rumors than face dangerous realities.

"Bock starts you off giggling, but leaves you with a chill."
– *Time Out New York*

"... a delightfully paranoid little nightmare that is both more chillingly realistic and pointedly absurd than anything John Grisham ever dreamed up."
– *New York Times*

SAMUELFRENCH.COM

NO SEX PLEASE, WE'RE BRITISH
Anthony Marriott and Alistair Foot

Farce / 7 m, 3 f / Interior

A young bride who lives above a bank with her husband who is the assistant manager, innocently sends a mail order off for some Scandinavian glassware. What comes is Scandinavian pornography. The plot revolves around what is to be done with the veritable floods of pornography, photographs, books, films and eventually girls that threaten to engulf this happy couple. The matter is considerably complicated by the man's mother, his boss, a visiting bank inspector, a police superintendent and a muddled friend who does everything wrong in his reluctant efforts to set everything right, all of which works up to a hilarious ending of closed or slamming doors. This farce ran in London over eight years and also delighted Broadway audiences.

"Titillating and topical."
– *NBC TV*

"A really funny Broadway show."
– *ABC TV*

SAMUELFRENCH.COM

OUTRAGE
Itamar Moses

Drama / 8m, 2f / Unit Set

In Ancient Greece, Socrates is accused of corrupting the young with his practice of questioning commonly held beliefs. In Renaissance Italy, a simple miller named Menocchio runs afoul of the Inquisition when he develops his own theory of the cosmos. In Nazi Germany, the playwright Bertolt Brecht is persecuted for work that challenges authority. And in present day New England, a graduate student finds himself in the center of a power struggle over the future of the University. An irreverent epic that spans thousands of years, *Outrage* explores the power of martyrdom, the power of theatre, and how the revolutionary of one era become the tyrant of the next.

WHITE BUFFALO
Don Zolidis

Drama / 3m, 2f (plus chorus)/ Unit Set
Based on actual events, WHITE BUFFALO tells the story of the miracle birth of a white buffalo calf on a small farm in southern Wisconsin. When Carol Gelling discovers that one of the buffalo on her farm is born white in color, she thinks nothing more of it than a curiosity. Soon, however, she learns that this is the fulfillment of an ancient prophecy believed by the Sioux to bring peace on earth and unity to all mankind. Her little farm is quickly overwhelmed with religious pilgrims, bringing her into contact with a culture and faith that is wholly unfamiliar to her. When a mysterious businessman offers to buy the calf for two million dollars, Carol is thrown into doubt about whether to profit from the religious beliefs of others or to keep true to a spirituality she knows nothing about.

SAMUELFRENCH.COM

BLUE YONDER
Kate Aspengren

Dramatic Comedy / Monolgues and scenes
12f (can be performed with as few as 4 with doubling) / Unit Set

A familiar adage states, "Men may work from sun to sun, but women's work is never done." In Blue Yonder, the audience meets twelve mesmerizing and eccentric women including a flight instructor, a firefighter, a stuntwoman, a woman who donates body parts, an employment counselor, a professional softball player, a surgical nurse professional baseball player, and a daredevil who plays with dynamite among others. Through the monologues, each woman examines her life's work and explores the career that she has found. Or that has found her.

SAMUELFRENCH.COM

www.ingramcontent.com/pod-product-compliance
Lightning Source LLC
Chambersburg PA
CBHW070645300426
44111CB00013B/2279